Another Bump in the Road
One Woman's Journey Through ALS

Leslie Shapiro
batlady@comcast.net

*Dedicated to the memory
of a
wonderful friend
and a
true inspiration*

Contents

Introduction

When my lifelong friend Linda Burge was diagnosed with Amyotrophic Lateral Sclerosis (ALS) in 1999 at the age of 51, it was an absolute shock. She was not going to recuperate. Lou Gehrig's disease is *always* fatal. When one is diagnosed with the dreaded "Big C," there is usually hope that it will be cured or go into remission, but there can be no such hope with ALS.

Yet Linda *was* hopeful. She fully understood that her disease was progressive and her disabilities would increase with time, but she was not going to allow a devastating diagnosis terminate her zest for life.

Linda displayed amazing fortitude and courage throughout her battle with ALS. She was a successful self-advocate and fought with great determination to retain her independence, as she lived alone for the duration of her illness. Linda faced this insidious disease with remarkable grace and acceptance. Despite everything she endured, she *never* complained, and there was *never* an inkling of self-pity. Linda steadfastly refused to see herself as a victim.

As I watched Linda through the beginning stages of her disease, I kept thinking that her experience should be documented in some way – interviews, video – something that would show others what an incredible role model she was. This idea gnawed at me continuously for the next few years, yet I never mentioned it to her. I was afraid she would be insulted by the invasion of privacy that would result from any public documentation of her battle with ALS.

In December of 2004, I read Mitch Albom's book, *Tuesdays with Morrie*. This is the true story of Mitch's former college professor, Morrie Schwartz, who had ALS. Mitch visited him every Tuesday, and was moved profoundly by Morrie's courage, philosophy, and exuberance for life.

As I read Albom's book, I was reminded constantly of Linda, but not because both she and Morrie shared the same disease. It was because both she and Morrie shared the same optimistic attitude about life, and despite the ravages of a fatal disease, neither of them would submit to defeat. Mitch talked about how Morrie's house always was filled with company – friends who had come to visit with Morrie because he was a joy to be with despite his illness. That was Linda! She had a busier social life than anybody I knew. People were frequently visiting her because she was a pleasure to be around. Though not a philosopher like Morrie, Linda was a gregarious person who had a genuine interest in each and every friend, loved girl talk, and lots of laughs. She made friends easily and had a wide circle of friends from all walks of life. A visit with Linda was a cheerful respite in anyone's day.

As Mitch was inspired by Morrie, so I was inspired by my dear friend. Albom's book was the impetus I needed to realize that if Linda's story was to be told, then *I* had to tell it. I knew what Linda had been through. I knew many of the obstacles she fought, and I have always felt that others could learn so much from her experiences. But... would she agree to a story written about her battle with ALS? By the time of my proposal, breathing had become an issue and it affected her speech. I wasn't sure if Linda would be up to the challenge of talking for long periods of time into a tape recorder, and I still worried that she would consider the idea an invasion of her privacy. I finally told her I wanted to document her illness and how she was dealing with it. I emphasized that in order to do this, she and I would have to sit for many interviews. Her response was, "Sure. Knock yourself out!"

I was taken aback by Linda's immediate and surprising answer. All the years before I had been so hesitant to broach the subject because I was certain she would consider it too invasive. I am sorry for those lost opportunities, but grateful that Linda agreed so readily when I did ask. She was an exceptionally articulate storyteller, blessed with a phenomenal memory. As a result, details had not escaped with time and every interview with Linda was precise, eloquent, and rich with information.

I had hoped, and I had truly believed, that I would complete this book with Linda's approval every step of the way. At the outset, I told Linda that I knew she did not want to be "defined" by her disease. She had a full life for 51 years before ALS introduced itself. Though the focus of the book was to show how valiantly Linda dealt with her illness, I also wanted to highlight the pre-ALS Linda in little vignettes throughout her life, enjoying herself and her friends during different periods. This would not be a biography, though we'd certainly get a clear picture of the pre and post ALS subject. Linda was in total agreement with that vision for the book presentation.

Since I was documenting Linda's experiences, I thought it was important to start off with an explanation of our relationship in the book. After a chapter centering around the two of us, I would begin the saga of Linda's "ALS Career" (as she often referred to it). Progression of the disease would be detailed chronologically. These chapters would be interspersed with others pertaining to various times in Linda's life as viewed by Linda or other family/friends. Linda approved this arrangement of chapters.

On many Saturdays, I went to Linda's with my faithful tape recorder, and suggest a topic for Linda to address. She would then expound on the topic – always in her meticulous and expressive fashion. Her brain was like a vault – she remembered everything in minute detail. Speaking for long periods of time was extremely difficult for her, but she was a trouper. Most days, she would go for about an hour before we'd have to stop.

When I returned home, I transcribed the interview on the computer. Then I e-mailed Linda a copy. She would make any changes or edits she deemed necessary, then e-mail the interview back to me.

After we had completed many interviews, I decided to write the first two chapters. I brought them to Linda's and read them to her.

She was pleased by what she heard. Though we had a very long way to go, those first chapters gave the book a life, and a reality beyond our weekly interviews.

That was in the summer of 2005. I fully expected that as I put together each chapter, Linda would either give her stamp of approval or make suggestions to improve what I presented. Though we continued with our Saturday interviews as the months went on, I was not able to write any additional specific chapters in the book because I was too busy with my job as an elementary school teacher.

Then the unthinkable happened. Linda died on January 21, 2006. I wasn't prepared. Regardless of her illness, it did not seem to be her time.

There was a very long period before I could do any work on the book. This was OUR project – Linda's and mine. To me it was essential that Linda approve all the information in the book, and that she have the last word on each chapter. Now, that was not going to happen. This became a solo project.

I had gotten enough material from Linda to write the book, but emotionally I couldn't look at it for a very long time. Though I had anticipated this as a venture we would celebrate together upon its completion and publication, it was now a labor of love that I would dedicate to the memory of my beloved friend.

ALS, also known as Amyotrophic Lateral Sclerosis, also known as Lou Gehrig's Disease, is a progressive, fatal neuromuscular disease. As nerve cells are destroyed, the patient eventually becomes paralyzed. Ultimately, even breathing becomes a struggle. New York Yankees Hall of Fame baseball player Lou Gehrig was diagnosed with ALS in 1939, and he died two years later at the age of 38. Today, there is still no known cause, treatment, or cure for the disease.

The title of this story, *Another Bump in the Road*, is in no way meant to minimize the seriousness of this horrific disease. Rather, it is a reflection of the relentless spirit of an extraordinary woman who refused to let the brutal obstacles related to this disease rob her of whatever quality of life she could muster under the circumstances.

This is the story of Linda's journey through ALS.

Chapter One
Hyannis Memories

Leslie:

It seems like Linda and I were friends all of our lives, but we actually met during our sophomore year at Brockton High School. We shared a locker in gym; however, it was our mutual adoration of Richard Chamberlain, TV's "Dr. Kildare," that drew us together as friends forever.

Maybe because we were both born under the sign of Taurus (I am 11 days older), we were very similar in personality. Both of us were good students, very responsible and dependable, loved to babysit when we were teens, and hung out with other kids who, like us, always walked the straight and narrow. Yep, by today's standards we were a boring duo, but we always had fun and enjoyed ourselves, never feeling the need to make mischief in order to have a good time. As typical teenagers, we were about a thousand years away from even thinking about our own mortality.

During one of our high school summers, a mutual friend had introduced us to Hyannis. Neither Linda nor I had ever been there, but Francie had an aunt who lived there during the summer months. Linda and I accompanied Francie and her family to her aunt's house one summer day, and we were hooked. Though both of us had spent appreciable time with our own families at various ocean areas, Hyannis had an intoxicating cachet – at least for the two of us. After all, this was the summer stomping ground of most of the Kennedy family. For two impressionable teenagers who both had scrapbooks of the President's young widow, traveling anywhere in Hyannis brought us closer to that mystique.

After our first visit with Francie's family, Hyannis became our favorite summer time haunt. Linda did not have her driver's license in high school, but I did. Oftentimes when my parents allowed me to take the car after they came home from work, I would pick up Linda and we'd cruise along the highway and be on the Cape and in Hyannis in 90 minutes. It did not take us long to establish a specific routine once we drove into town. We always stopped at the Kennedy Memorial off Lewis Bay. We would walk to the fountain, stay a few minutes, then get back into the car and head for the Kennedy compound. In those days there were always police officers a block away from the compound to prevent any unauthorized vehicles, which translated into any and all tourists and oglers, from entering the area. Not once, in our many trips to Hyannis – and we *always* drove to the compound – did we ever penetrate that well-guarded block. We never expected to get into the hallowed fortress, but it gave us pleasure just to creep along the outskirts.

From the compound, we'd drive to downtown Hyannis, where street parking was at a premium. Most of the time, we would pull into the back parking lot of the big department store on Main Street to save us the aggravation of scouting for nonexistent street parking. Linda and I loved to walk leisurely along Main Street and browse the many quaint shops. The glass blowers at work in front of the fine glass shop would often beckon us to watch them as they created their magic with liquid glass. It was nearly impossible to walk past the fudge shop without sampling the wares. Then there were clothing shops, gift shops, the book store, the peanut store, and countless others that we felt deserved our attention. Linda and I did not buy a lot, but we loved to look.

After about an hour or so of covering all of Main Street on foot, we would take off for our two favorite gift shops – The Barefoot Trader and Treasure Island. They were both a good distance from the downtown area, and worth the trip because they were humungous stores with lots of unique items. Perusing both shops would take at least another hour, and by that time it would be rather late. No trip to Hyannis would be complete without a visit to Four Seas Ice Cream Parlor, which is actually in Centerville, right next to Hyannis. This ice cream parlor is the oldest on the Cape and has been in operation since 1934. It is legendary because of its old fashioned atmosphere and its fabulous ice cream. Linda and I would often savor those wonderful flavors while sitting on Craigville Beach, just a short drive from Four Seas.

Nearly every trip to Hyannis followed this same pattern, and we never tired of it. However, Linda recalls another trip that was an aberration from our usual routine.

~~~~~~~~~~~~~~~~~~~~~~~~~~~~

Linda:
I remember one Saturday night when we were in high school and I was babysitting. Leslie was at home and we were on the phone chatting. It was a beautiful night. The parents I was babysitting for were expected home by midnight. Leslie and I planned for her to pick me up at my house after I got home and then we'd drive to Hyannis in the middle of the night, hang out for awhile, have breakfast later on, and then return home. We had planned to watch the sun come up over the ocean.

When I got home from babysitting, I went in and woke up my mother, and said, "Leslie is coming to pick me up. We're going to Hyannis. I'll be home in the morning."

Well, my father sat straight up and said, "Are you out of your mind?"

I just said, "No, it will be fun, and we'll be fine."

My mother said to my dad, "I can't stop her. It's what she wants to do." Then she turned to me and said, "Be careful."

Looking back I am sure my father probably bitched at my mother all night!

Leslie picked me up and we drove to Hyannis. There were no cars on the road, and it was a great ride. We were typical teenagers in the car - fast driving, the wind in our hair, and the feeling of freedom. Once in Hyannis, we rode all around to the different

3

beaches, and we stopped at the Kennedy Memorial. No one was around and we rode all over the place. We walked on the beach – either Craigville or Sea Street. We watched the sun come up, and then we went to the Pancake Man for breakfast. We were back in Brockton by about 8 AM. Leslie dropped me off and my dad was still ticked! He was out front washing the car. I said hi and he looked at me like, "You're a pain in my butt!" however, he didn't actually say anything. I went in the house and went to bed.

~~~~~~~~~~~~~~~~~~~~~~~~

Linda - recollecting our first overnight weekend visit in Hyannis:

Someone I worked with in high school told me about a guest house in Hyannis that was highly recommended. It was well run and very clean. It was the equivalent of a bed and breakfast without the breakfast. It had a shared bath. I know my mother was concerned about us staying there, and I remember she actually called and talked to the owner. Anyway, it was lovely – immaculate and comfortable. Leslie and I went for a weekend and stayed there. That was the first of a handful of weekenders in Hyannis.

It seems like on those weekend sleepovers, we always followed a favorite routine – we'd shop, go to the Music Circus (outdoor entertainment under a big tent), and go to our favorite gift shops. We were kids and we were on a budget, but we always had a great time.

One time we had a big weekend planned in Hyannis that did not turn out as expected! We planned a day boat trip to Nantucket, followed by dinner at a nice restaurant back in Hyannis, and then after dinner, we had tickets for the Music Circus. On the return trip back to Hyannis, the ferry ran aground! We were stuck for a while and they ended up having to unload everyone onto another boat. As a result, we missed our reservations for dinner, but we made the show at the Music Circus. I don't remember what we saw that night, but we did see several Broadway musicals at the Music Circus like "Funny Girl" and "Oliver."

When we did see "Funny Girl" on a Saturday night, the very next day, the star of the show, Barbara Minsky, happened to come into the deli on Main St. in Hyannis where we were eating breakfast. We thought it was a riot because in the show she had this cute little white dog, and when she came into the deli, she had the same dog with her!

Another Hyannis adventure I recall is once when we had gone down to the Kennedy compound and Leslie had gone through a stop sign. A police officer on foot was running after her blowing his whistle. He gave Leslie a citation and she was very upset. She was concerned that her father would be pretty mad. However, later Leslie told me that her fears were laid to rest because when she told her dad what happened, he just laughed!

Looking back on it I think for kids in those times, the 60s, we were really quite adventurous and quite responsible. We both had our own part time jobs. We were not mooching off our parents. We were able to finance these little getaways ourselves. My parents did not give me money for them and neither did Leslie's.

I cannot recall any other friends who were so adventurous and went off like that on their own at that age – at least none of my friends did. I never felt uneasy, apprehensive, or nervous when we traveled. We had a lot of fun. Never saw any Kennedys - but we never gave up trying!

Chapter 2
First Symptoms

Linda:

In March of 1998 I was at my friend Gail's for a brunch along with another friend, Peggy. A family emergency came up and Gail had to leave. I said to Peggy, "I can't make a fist with my left hand." Peggy laughed and said, "It's a good thing because you'll avoid fisticuffs with anyone!"

This was my first conscious awareness that something was neurologically not quite right with my body. However, my ability to make a fist came back, so I was not too concerned.

(Note: At this time Linda was working two full time jobs. The year before, Linda worked at Commonwealth Mortgage Co. on the North Shore. She lost this position when the company closed the office in late winter of '97. It was during this time that Linda was convalescing from a broken ankle and had been out of work for a couple of months. After her ankle healed, she worked full time for Wal-Mart, then got an additional full time position at the South Shore Cooperative Bank in May, '98. So as of May, '98, she was working two full time jobs, days, nights, and weekends, for about 70-80 hours every week.)

My initial symptoms were in my left hand. Shortly after the episode at Gail's, I noticed sporadic weakness in my left hand. If I was completely relaxed, like when watching TV or reading, the finger next to my pinky started twitching uncontrollably.

As the symptoms started to manifest themselves in the beginning, I thought it might be fatigue, though I became more aware of fine motor skills failing me as well. From time to time, I was having difficulty counting money at Wal-Mart. Every night I had to print reports from the computer and hang them on a corkboard. When I went to put up the tack with my right hand, I couldn't press the pin through the paper and into the corkboard. I realized this was a red flag, indicating something was really wrong.

Also around this time, I had some unexplained falls, and I was easily knocked off balance. One day at Wal-Mart, a little child ran into me and I fell right down. I also fell in the office at the bank a couple of times. I kept thinking the reason for all these falls had to be the broken ankle.

However, something significant occurred that proved to me this was more serious. One night in the summer of '98, I was trying to insert my key into the mailbox and I couldn't do it. I also had this same struggle opening my front door. The only way I could manage was to use two hands to manipulate the key. At that point, I knew I had a neurological problem.

I began to make a lot of adjustments – relocating things at work, like file drawers, making gradual accommodations that allowed me to function without the issues.

During this time ('98), co-workers at Wal-Mart noticed the difficulty I had trying to unlock the cash vault drawers and asked if something was wrong with my hand.

"Why are you holding the key like that?" (I put the key between my knuckles so I could hold it.)

One day the assistant manager noticed my trouble as I was ringing a register and bagging. He realized I was slowing down the line, and he said, "You ring, I'll bag." Later he asked me about it. I told him there was something wrong, I was aware of it, and I was trying to get a medical appointment.

My boss at the bank noticed I was having problems handling papers and writing. As a young man, he suffered with severe arthritis and he said, "I think you're developing arthritis. I'll get you an appointment with my arthritis doctor." I said, "Fine, that's a good place to start." However, his doctor wouldn't see me without a referral because it would be a waste of the doctor's time if it was not arthritis.

(*Note: In 1973, Linda was diagnosed with Multiple Sclerosis. Since the time of her diagnosis, she had no further symptoms of the disease.*)

It crossed my mind that MS symptoms were finally manifesting themselves. They told me back in '73 that some people with MS have symptoms that continue to progress, some people have symptoms that occur at intervals, and some people have symptoms that may occur only once.

During my lunch break at work at the bank one day, I was reading an article in a magazine about Jennifer Estes, a young woman with ALS, and I began to think that maybe I have ALS, though it still seemed more likely it was the MS.

My health insurance was user friendly. I could go anywhere, anytime without a referral, but the specialists I called wouldn't see me without a referral. Finally I called my primary care doctor's office in November and said I needed to see my doctor for a check up. I was given an appointment for April. After I hung up I realized what a big mistake I had made. Waiting until April was ridiculous, so I called back and said, "Listen, I have a serious problem. My symptoms appear to be neurological and I am losing muscle control and falling. I can't wait until April. I need to see the doctor for about ten minutes for him to give me a referral." I then got an appointment for Jan. 4, 1999, which was 7-8 weeks away, not great, but a whole lot better than waiting for five months.

Chapter 3
Diagnosis

Linda:

On January 4, 1999, I saw my primary care physician, and the first thing he said was, "What brings you here?" I said, "I'm losing my grip," and showed him how I could not make a fist with either hand. I also told him my fingers were curling up on a regular basis. "I think I have a brain tumor, the Multiple Sclerosis is presenting itself after all these years, or I have a spinal tumor." The idea of a spinal tumor was terrifying to me, and it was my biggest fear.

The doctor did a quick neurological exam and said he didn't think it was any of the things I had suggested, but he thought it involved my neck. All the messages from the brain pass through the neck at the top of the spine and are transmitted to where they need to go. He believed something at my neck was stopping brain signals from getting through and he thought ALS was likely. It was almost a relief to hear him say ALS because the idea of any cancer terrifies me, having seen my mother go through the gates of hell with her cancer (liver, spleen, pancreatic). Since he was not a specialist, he referred me to a neurologist for testing. My appointment would be the following week. Apparently, now the door was open and I was on the fast track! For months I had been trying to see *any* doctor, now I was getting right through.

The neurologist was local - in Weymouth. This doctor gave me a neurological exam in the office and said he did not believe it was MS or a brain tumor. The symptoms pointed to ALS, but more tests were needed to confirm a diagnosis. I saw him many times in quick succession in a period of less than two weeks. He set up an MRI, had me come in for a spinal tap and an EMG. (An EMG is an Electromyogram which is electrical testing of nerves and muscles.)

I went as an outpatient to the South Shore Hospital for the EMG. I was not really prepared for what was to come. Having no preconceived idea, I was not nervous. I think I expected something like an EKG, which is not painful. For some reason, on that day, the room was hot and my body was also hot. The doctor wanted my skin temperature to be cooler. He filled the sink in the exam room with cold water and had me stand by the sink, leaning into it on my elbows with my lower arms emerged for several minutes. It was so odd and awkward for me to be standing like that. However, it did cool me off. It was the middle of winter, and I had probably come dressed in a warm sweater. The test involved electric stimulation and invasive needles, but it was limited. He did my forearms, a little on my shoulders and neck, and my upper arms. The test was quite painful, but it was of limited scope and time.

At the end of all these tests he said he was 90% sure that I had ALS. He also said he wasn't an expert in ALS, and this type of diagnosis warranted a second expert opinion. He referred me to Dr. David Weinberg at St. Elizabeth's Medical Center in Boston.

In January '99 I got right in to see Dr. Weinberg, and there were many, many appointments in quick succession. It was very in-depth testing and a lot of blood work was done because there are numerous neurological diseases, some of which are quite treatable (like Lyme disease, mercury poisoning, viruses, etc.)

He set up a full body EMG that I will never forget. I expected it to be similar to the torture I endured at Weymouth. I got through that, so I expected, as bad as it was, I could do it again. I thought, "It won't be fun, but I will get through it." I did not realize that it was a whole body test and it took hours.

The test is two parts. First, they attach electrodes all over and zap you all over to see how your nerves and muscles react. It's very unpleasant, but I could deal with it. Second, they take wire hook-shaped needles that are attached to electric wires and attach these to parts of your body. Then they tell you to push or pull. The feedback goes through the wires and measures how your muscles and nerves react. It was very painful. The whole test took about three hours. We took a break between part one and part two.

I remember at one point, after a 15 minute break, I was rolled on my side. The doctor was working on the backs of my legs (thigh and calf muscles), and tears began to roll from my eyes. This was not an emotional reaction, but a reaction to the intense pain. The doctor said if I couldn't go on I could come back and we'd do it another day.

I said, "No, I would never be able to do this again. It's now or never."

When I sat up after the test, I noticed many spots of blood all over the sheet. I said, "I'm sorry, I really had a hard time."

He said, "You did great! Most people never get through the whole thing. Many patients scream and yell."

The tests were extraordinarily painful and emotionally disconcerting.

Dr. Weinberg continued to see me for a few more appointments where he did in-office neurological exams, and he was evaluating all the tests. (All the testing was done during January and February '99.) The results seemed to eliminate everything else, so it appeared to be ALS. He suggested a nerve biopsy on my foot. He did not satisfy me that it would be any more conclusive or that it would show more than previous tests had shown. He also mentioned that I would probably be left with a permanent numbness in that area of my foot. He did not seem to be pushing for this test, and after much discussion, we mutually decided not to do the test. He felt he had enough information to make a final diagnosis which I discussed with him in early March.

In discussing my diagnosis, Dr. Weinberg was very calm and empathetic as he confirmed that the tests indicated I had ALS. I began to cry when he said this, but I believe the motivation for the tears was not just the bad news, but an emotional release at finally having a diagnosis. He was understanding of my reaction. We were in his office library, and he walked across the room, gave me a tissue, put an arm around my shoulder, and gave me time to release and vent. He said, "You've been through so much, just take your time." Then he set up another appointment a few days later so we could discuss a plan of action.

With ALS, the term is not "treatment," it is "disease management." Dr. Weinberg recommended dietary supplements, medication, physical therapy, and getting voice recognition software. He prescribed Rilutek, which is the only FDA approved drug for the treatment of ALS. (In some cases it's believed to slow down the progression minimally – up to 10% of the normal rate.) He advised me to supplement my diet with 2,000 units of vitamin E, 300 milligrams of CO-Q10, a vitamin B complex, calcium with magnesium, and a regular multi-vitamin. I've been taking this regimen ever since. (He also prescribed creatine, but I discontinued it early on because of digestive discomfort.)

Dr. Weinberg sent me to 21 physical therapy sessions at South Shore Hospital. The physical therapy gave me benefits that were both physical and psychological. In addition, I learned a regimen of exercises I could continue on my own at home. I also saw an occupational therapist there who gave me some equipment that helped at home, such as a button hook, a long shoehorn, and a special cutting board. These were little things that were a big help.

Over the next few months I had follow up visits with Dr. Weinberg, and on one of these visits I asked him point blank for a prognosis. He said statistically, 80% of ALS patients die within 1-2 years of their diagnosis. Because I was in good health other than the ALS, he estimated I had a year or maybe more.

I stopped working at Wal-Mart in March, '99. My primary physician said he'd rather see me walk a mile around the track at the high school, than run around Wal-Mart. (It was shortly after this that I quit Wal-Mart.)

Drug Study

In the summer of '99 Dr. Weinberg made me aware of a drug study at the Lahey Clinic (in Burlington, MA), and he thought I'd be an excellent candidate. I was accepted as a participant. My motivation for entering the study was not because I held out any hope for myself, but because I thought the results might benefit future ALS patients. The drug being tested was Topiramate, an anti-seizure drug used on epileptics. Researchers thought it could have some kind of beneficial effects on ALS. This was a blind study with a limited number of participants. A small number would receive the drug and everyone else would receive a placebo. Dr. James Russell was leading the study. Before starting the study the participants were given paper work that informed them of all possible side effects of the drug. I did not read it because I did not want to prejudice myself. I started taking what I assumed was the placebo. Within a couple of days I started falling repeatedly, suffered with vertigo and dizziness, had exaggerated ALS symptoms, and felt very sick with all these symptoms. I called Dr. Russell and told him I was concerned because the ALS symptoms seemed to be out of control. He said that everything I was experiencing were textbook side effects of the drug, and he thought I must be getting the drug. (He did not know which patients had the drug and which had the placebo.) The dosage was 25 milligrams the first week, doubling every successive week until you reached 800 milligrams. Based on the problems I was having, he decided to hold my dose at the initial 25 milligrams indefinitely to see if I'd adjust. After a couple of weeks, I was feeling better. The problems seemed to have subsided back to pre-drug, ALS status, so Dr. Russell increased the dosage to 50 milligrams. Right away I went into a tailspin that was even worse than the initial dosage. This was right before Christmas of '99. Christmas eve day at work I fell, and then I fell twice at home. I was hardly able to walk. I could not reach the doctor. I had asked him once before if I could stop the drug without weaning off of it, and he said yes. Thus, I made the decision that I was done. I took a limo to my sister's house in NH for Christmas. When my sister and brother-in-law saw me, they were worried because I looked visibly weakened and I was hardly able to walk.

(Note: The entire drug study terminated early. Some patients, like Linda, had very negative reactions and withdrew early. Some patients had no reactions at all. Some patients got sicker, some showed a little improvement. The overall results were inconclusive and no further study was made on that drug.)

During the period I participated in the drug study, I found that Dr. Russell and I were not a match made in heaven. We just did not hit it off. I thought that in his eyes, I was nothing more than a laboratory rat. He did not treat me like a physician normally treats a patient. I felt he had a cold and irritating bedside manner. Dealing with him was very frustrating. When I finally dropped out of the study, his secretary called me a few days later to invite me to become his permanent patient. My response was: "Not if he was the last doctor on earth!" And that ended that conversation.

When I dropped out of the drug study, Dr. Russell called me to say thank you and goodbye. I asked him point blank, what he saw as a prognosis. In his cool, and what I considered an offensive manner, he said, "I am not going to candy coat this. You are an intelligent woman. I give you six months to a year." I thought, "I did not ask you that," but it's the way he interpreted my question. Actually, what I was asking was, "What should I expect or anticipate happening in my future?"

A couple of weeks later I had my usual appointment with Dr. Weinberg. He and Dr. Russell were not only colleagues, they were friends, which is how Dr. Weinberg knew about the study and got me in. I told Dr. Weinberg that I really did not hit it off with Dr. Russell. I explained that I was done with the study, and related what the problems had been. Dr. Weinberg totally supported my decision to drop out. When I told him what I had said to Dr. Russell's secretary, he laughed, but he was also concerned. Dr. Weinberg said he had never heard anyone with such a negative opinion of Dr. Russell. He was perplexed at the emotional barrier between me and his colleague. Despite that barrier, Dr. Weinberg encouraged me to make an appointment with Dr. Russell for numerous persuasive reasons.

He explained that if I availed myself of disease follow up and management under the auspices of the MDA/ALS clinic at the Lahey, I would benefit from many advantages that could not be duplicated at his hospital, St. Elizabeth's. The MDA clinic offers supervision by an ALS specialist (Dr. Russell), physical therapy, occupational therapy, and a social worker. It makes available a great deal of information to the patient and caregivers and it facilitates patient visits because it is like "one stop shopping" - you can see many of the health care providers in one place at the time you are there.

There were also insurance advantages: certain treatments and equipment are covered by insurance under the auspices of Dr. Russell and the MDA. If I continued at St. Elizabeth's these things would not be covered. Dr. Weinberg said he wanted to continue to be my doctor when I needed him, and he would follow my case with Dr. Russell. However, for my own convenience and financial well-being, I would be better off at Lahey. Dr. Weinberg assured me he was not throwing me out! I could continue with him if Dr. Russell and MDA did not satisfy my needs.

Dr. Weinberg's arguments for the MDA clinic at the Lahey were too compelling for me to ignore, so I called and made an appointment with Dr. Russell. One of my friends accompanied me on that first visit. I think it was Betsy. At the initial meeting as a patient, not as a drug study participant, Dr. Russell's attitude was completely different. (It may have been partially because his friend Dr. Weinberg said something to him.) Since that time, Dr. Russell has been supportive and encouraging.

Now, Dr. Russell always says he should have pulled me out immediately from the drug study when I had such an initial bad reaction. He also frequently refers to the time he did not give me that long to live. Often he will have a student with him and he'll tell the student that I am his best resource. He takes lots of notes on me about what I have acquired in the way of services, equipment, etc., and he passes this information along to other patients.

Chapter 4
Family Reaction to Diagnosis

Linda:

I have a small family, and my sister Judy was very supportive initially. She wrote me a beautiful letter about her and her husband John's willingness and intent to support me in this, which they have. I have chosen not to burden them, but when I have needed them and asked, they have always been there.

At the time of my diagnosis, they were building a new home to which they added a ramp and a guest room and bath that were handicap accessible. The idea of my living with them was more or less an understanding or an assumption that when I could no longer work and get along without assistance, I would be welcomed in their home. As time went on, my brother-in-law John had some health issues. My sister had a big challenge trying to deal emotionally with his serious illness. I realized that living with them would be a disservice to them and to me.

Without my asking her to, Judy began to research nursing homes. At the same time, I was also doing a similar investigation. Eventually she found a place in NH she thought would be just wonderful. I told her at the time that if and when I ever need a residential care setting, I had decided to remain in MA. Clearly, it made the most sense. If I moved to NH, my sister, brother-in-law, and their daughter would be the only ones who would feel compelled to visit me in the home. Here in MA, I have so many friends who visit me now in my condo. All my friends were upset and very much against my moving to NH. They all said they would not be able to visit me in NH, but here, they could continue to be part of my life.

I did not know at the time, but I know now that when I got a confirmed diagnosis, my sister went on the internet and looked up anything and everything she could find about ALS. I understand she was trying to educate herself. It was a crash course, and it was, I believe, emotionally overwhelming for her. I think at the time, the overexposure of information put her in a mind set of "My sister has ALS. My sister is dead." I don't think she understood that there *was*, and still *is* for me, a big distance between becoming ill and the end of life. I have had over five years of many, many happy occasions, parties, outings, meetings with friends, and wonderful times. It took my sister a while, a *long* while, to be able to see me as someone *living* with ALS, who is still able to find enjoyment in life.

Her daughter Susan, my adult niece to whom I was very close, did not believe the diagnosis. Right away she was looking for other answers, coming up with many different suggestions. Though she understood that I had been tested and tested and tested by three excellent specialists, it took awhile for her to finally believe their universal diagnosis was correct.

Interestingly, my great niece, Melissa, and her brother Chris were teenagers at the time of my initial diagnosis. Chris actually was ten. They both pretty much rolled with it. I remember Melissa saying to me, "You may be crooked, but you are still my Auntie Linda!" She was about 14 or 15 at that time. However, now that she is 21, she has a hard time with it. Melissa and I used to be very close, and now I seldom hear from her. She never comes to visit, and she has told my sister (her grandmother) that she just cannot deal with it.

Most people have trouble dealing with a devastating disease. I think they often forget that you are still the same person, whether you are in a wheelchair, or your speech is distorted, and no matter how much you are physically changed, you are still the same person. Chris Reeve's book was subtitled *I'm Still Me*. That book and its title really inspired me. I also think many people allow themselves to be defined by their illness, and I have fought every step of the way <u>not</u> to let ALS define me.

It is very hard for people to whom you are close to accept bad news of any kind. Different people had different reactions to my diagnosis. There was more than one who said, "Maybe they're wrong. Maybe it's a mistake. Maybe you should see another doctor." If I had not seen three specialists from three different hospitals, I might have had that same feeling. But having been through all the tests three times, with three different major medical leaders, I had no doubt. I have been fortunate that all of my family and all of my friends have stuck with me and carried on our relationships as normally as we can. Some have brought meals to my home to share, while others have cooked meals for me in my home. Friends visit to watch movies, play Scrabble, or just have some laughs. Occasionally we will go out together to a restaurant or whatever. As my friend Patty once said, "There has not been a deserter in the bunch." Everyone has stood by me and not excluded me from their lives in any way.

The relationship with my sister has changed in some ways these last few years. I feel comfortable in it now, though it took me awhile. Up until my parents died and then I got sick shortly thereafter, I think my sister and I had a very good relationship, but it was based on having fun together, going places, holidays, parties, etc. Because of what we went through with my parents' deaths, and then the ALS diagnosis, our relationship had to adjust and become a bond that would withstand things that are not fun, and it took time for that to evolve. I believe part of the reason was because I, trying to be very independent, went out of my way to prevent my sister from seeing what my life is really like. I protected her – shielded her from the not so pretty aspects of ALS, and it took a long time before she would (or could) reach out to help me and do things like feed me. In her defense, I never asked for her help. I realize she was probably hesitant to overstep or push, and I complicated the matter by telling her, "I don't need help." At this point in time, our relationship status has settled and we are both comfortable with her providing me with whatever help she can handle. I've never asked her to do any personal care, but she can help me with some things.

I think the Cliff Walk (*a major fundraiser sponsored by the ALS Charitable Foundation in which participants get sponsors and walk seven miles along the canal in Buzzards Bay, MA*) was a big breakthrough for her and me and our ALS relationship. When I first wanted to do the Cliff Walk fundraiser, I sent out letters to all my friends with the information, inviting them to take part and urging them to try to raise money for the charity. I approached my sister and her immediate response was that they would not attend. I was crushed. She said she could make a donation, but she could not ask anyone else to donate because she was uncomfortable asking people for money. We were talking on the phone. She and I never, never argue, but at that time, we came as close to an argument as we ever have. I remember she asked me what I expected from her, and I said, "Your support." She was furious. She said that I was hurtful, that she and her husband had always supported me and that it was very hurtful that I would say that. She told me I had offended her by asking for support. She took it that I was saying they did not support me. That was NOT what I said. I only asked for support for the Cliff Walk endeavor. I did tell her that I would pay for a hotel for them and their daughter and son-in-law and grandchildren if they would come down, stay overnight and attend the Cliff Walk. She said that was not necessary. She said she could not walk. She's very out of shape and has some issues with her legs. I said, "All you need to do is be a cheerleader. Sit on the sidelines. Trust me, most people will not walk, and if they do, they'll only walk a short way. It's a fundraiser. It's a gathering. It's a picnic and an awareness event."

Anyway, the conversation did not go well. We both hung up. I know she was hurt. I know I was hurt. I made up my mind not to mention it again. Several weeks passed and out of the blue, she told me that they would all be at the Cliff Walk. I was thrilled, and I let her know how much that meant to me. That first walk I believe I had about 50 people in my group – "Linda's Lucky Charms" – all with T-shirts - and it meant so much to me that my family did take part. I believe what it did – especially for Judy – was take away a lot of her fear of ALS. She saw a lot of people with family members in wheelchairs. People who were there just like she was, just like all of my friends, and she was face to face with others in the same position. In a way it was kind of like a group therapy experience, and she enjoyed the day thoroughly. The Cliff Walk is a fun event – very upbeat, very positive, and everyone in my family had a good time. I think that first event was a big breakthrough and a bridge to reconnect me and my sister with our current circumstances.

Chapter 5
Time to Move

Linda:

While I was participating in the drug study, it became more and more difficult for me to live in my townhouse. One evening on my way upstairs to my bedroom I got stuck halfway up the stairs – I could not go up, I could not go down. I sat down on the stairway and I fully thought I would be there for the weekend. I was expecting no one, and I thought, "Great, Monday morning they'll miss me in the office!" It was very frightening. I had a set of crutches at the top of the stairs and a set of crutches at the bottom, plus one that I was using to try to ascend the stairs, but I could not move. I rested on the stairs for a considerable period, trying not to panic. Ultimately, I thought my best shot would be to try to go down on my butt, and hopefully, when I got to the bottom, I would be able to pull myself up, grab the crutches, and either get to a chair or get to a phone. I did all of that. I got to the bottom, got the crutches, and managed to take a couple of steps to a nearby chair in my living room and just sit. I sat in that chair for hours. Then I thought I would try one more time to ascend the stairs, and I was able to do so. I had rallied! It probably was not a very wise move, but I did it.

At that time I waited for a sign about every decision I would have to make about my new life. I had been doing research on assisted living, which in no way could I afford. The fees are phenomenal. I knew I could not continue living in a multi-level home. I talked to Dr. Weinberg about the possibility of moving to a one level condo and I asked him if it would even be worth it. I told him I had a big condo full of collectibles, a million things to pack and discard and a move would be a major undertaking. When he asked me what would make it worthwhile I said to him - and this was December,

21

'99 - that if I could move and have three months of independent living it would be worth it. He said to me, "Start packing. I believe you might have six months or a year." I called a realtor and put my condo on the market. The first weekend we had an open house and my condo sold! Now I had to find a place to live very quickly. I had criteria for location, and of course it had to be one level, etc. Within two weeks, the realtor found my current home.

On January 20, 2000, I moved. Preparations for the move were quite an experience. Friends helped weed through my belongings and discard whatever. I hired packers. My family came from NH to help me with the move. They stayed in a motel for two nights. When they decided they needed to return home I had 21 unpacked boxes building a wall in my living room. I started unpacking little by little. Gail helped, and Patty helped. Different friends would come in and one by one we unpacked. My family helped with a lot of boxes as well. There were about 100 boxes all together. It was an amazing undertaking, but I finally got settled. The night after the initial move when my family had gone home, I was in my new living room and I got up onto my feet with my crutches to change the channel on my TV (no remote). When I leaned over, I fell, knocking my eye on the corner of the table. I immediately thought, "Have I made a mistake?" I managed to pull myself up on the chair and just sat there for a long time, trying to breathe.

It took a few weeks to get ship shape. I had downsized so significantly, but with the help of friends and with constant diligent effort on my own behalf, little by little, every dish, every knick knack, and everything else found a place.

It's my personal belief that timing is everything in life. I tried always to look ahead at the changes I would need to make, but at the same time, not to jump the gun – to wait for the time to be right. Just like moving. I could have rushed to move the day of the diagnosis, but I wanted to stay in my original home as long as I could and I waited for a sign. Getting stuck on the stairs was that sign.

Mom Keeps an Eye Out

I was out of work for a couple of weeks to accomplish the move. My company gave me the time off. It was a very snowy, very icy period. The night before I moved we had an ice storm and I was so afraid I'd fall walking into my new condo on moving day. I needed to have a railing put on the three steps in front of the condo to help me go in and out. I had arranged for that to be installed. I also arranged for a locksmith to put a new door handle on the front door, as I was unable to grasp the traditional rounded doorknob.

After the move, I was stuck in the house, settling in for a couple of weeks. The snow fell and melted, and fell and melted.

Finally I was ready to return to work, and my friend Fran, who was driving me, came to pick me up. Fran walked ahead of me and went down the stairs. I was holding my new railing and had a crutch under my right arm. As I looked down beside the stairway, I almost fainted! With a very sharp intake of breath I said, "Oh my God!"

Fran turned around. "What's wrong?"

I said, "My mother was here." On the ground around the shrubs beside the stairway were seashells and polished stones that had not been there previously. I had been in and out of this house with the realtor; I had been in and out on moving day. They had *not* been there. Now they were there!

My mother, when she was living at her own home, had an area near her front door where water dripped off the roof overhang and eroded the soil. She could not get anything to grow in that area. She tried gutters; she tried all kinds of things. The water always hit that spot. My mother, "the artist," could not be satisfied with no flowers, no grass, no shrubbery in that little area, so she started collecting colorful stones and seashells at the beach and filling in the area with a little stone garden. We called it "Dolly's Drip," because the water would drip off and make a very soothing tinkling sound as it hit the stones, and they would sparkle. Everyone who entered her house would notice them and comment.

23

If small children came to visit, they were attracted instantly by the seashells. If my mother liked the children, she would let them take a shell or two to keep. Here I was walking out my front door in my new place and all of a sudden on the ground right next to my doorway are shells and stones. My first thought was that my friend Gail, who was like a daughter to my mother, had put them there. That would be a typical Gail thing to do. I called Gail and her reply was, "Oh my God, if I had thought of it, I would have! It's like a miracle." There was no logical explanation for this. I truly believe that *somehow* my mother's spirit placed those rocks to let me know that she was here to watch over me. I called my sister and told her and she was completely overcome. She said it just gave her chills because there was no explanation. It was one of those spiritual encounters. It could have been a very frightening experience, but for me it was very reassuring, very warm. I know it sounds off the wall, but I have witnesses!

~~~~~~~~~~~~~~~~~~~~~~~~~

Angels on My Shoulder

My mother died in October of '95. When Christmas came up, my father was still grieving so deeply that he did not want to celebrate the holidays. I wanted to find a card for him that would express, "I'm your daughter, I love you." I looked at every Hallmark card and at every American Greetings card, but could not find what I wanted. One day I was working at Wal-Mart cleaning up around the front registers. I was picking up discards that people had decided they didn't want at the checkout. While sorting these items I picked up several individual Christmas cards. I turned one over and the card said, "To Dad from your daughter." Inside it said, "I love you at Christmas and every day of the year." That was all it said, no Merry Xmas, no Happy Holidays. It was *exactly* what I wanted, and at that very moment, I turned around because I felt like my mother was right behind me. One of my co-workers said to me, "Are you all right? You look like you've seen a ghost." And I said, "Well I didn't see one, but she was here." Of course, I purchased the card. I truly believe my mother had put that card into my hands.

~~~~~~~~~~~~~~~~~~~~~~~~~

A few months after I moved into my new condo, I was struggling with many issues. My daily life was becoming extremely difficult, and trying to deal with everything required great effort. I went to bed feeling quite exhausted. One time I awoke in the middle of the night, and an overwhelming scent filled my bedroom. It brought me back to when I was about four years of age when my dad, the milkman, would come home from work, smelling his own special scent of work, sweat, sour milk, Tide laundry detergent, and his Old Spice after shave. It was his scent. I thought I dreamed it. I got up, made my way to the bathroom, used the toilet, washed my hands, and had a glass of water. The scent was not present in the bathroom. I went back into the bedroom, and the scent surrounded me. Right out loud I said, "Thanks, Dad, I know you are here," and the scent went away immediately. I have no explanation, but I believe my father was there. I don't know why or how. Those experiences reinforce to me that God made angels surround me, and they're probably in the form of my parents.

~~~~~~~~~~~~~~~~~~~~~~~~~~~

After my move, I started hiring people to come to the condo to help me get up in the morning and into bed at night. However, it was not long before I lost a couple of my helpers. One was getting me up every day, and she was a sister to one of my other helpers who put me to bed a few nights a week. Their mother became very ill, and they had to leave to care for her. I was feeling very much against the wall because I not only needed to replace them, but I needed to think about replacing my dear friend Fran as well. Fran had been coming a few nights a week to put me to bed. However, she was not trained, and as my needs were growing, it was becoming too difficult for her.

I did not advertise for help. Instead, I was depending on word of mouth, but passing the word was not finding anyone. One day I was sitting at home and I was really down about it. I felt hopeless, and I didn't know where I would find the help I needed. I was praying and praying, and praying for help. All of a sudden, a light bulb went on in my head and I remembered my hairdresser knew a Chilean woman and her twin daughters, who were all certified nurses' aides. They lived right here in Rockland, too. I called Gina, my hairdresser, and asked if she thought they might be interested in helping me out. She gave me their phone number, and that very afternoon I had engaged the mother and the twin daughters to fill in the gaps. In this process I lost two sisters, but gained another two, plus their mom! Again, help came just when I needed it and when I had surrendered myself to God asking for assistance.

Chapter 6
Taiwan

Linda thought I was extremely gutsy to go to a college that was three thousand miles away from home (UCLA). She went to a two year secretarial school in Boston, followed by full time work at a bank in Brockton. However, my cross country status seemed like a stone's throw from home compared to the new adventure that fell into her lap and landed her half a world away.

Linda:

In 1968, I was 21 years old, living at home with my parents and working as a clerk in the accounting department of Plymouth-Home National Bank. I had friends, but no boyfriend, and all in all, I led a pretty quiet life. I remember feeling shy in social situations at that time.

My mother's brother Ed, a U.S. Army Lt. Colonel, came to visit my family before being deployed to a dangerous one year combat tour in Viet Nam. Uncle Ed, his wife, Aunt Betty, and their eight year-old daughter Ginny were stationed in Taipei, Taiwan for a number of years. They resided off base in a lovely home in a Chinese neighborhood. Aunt Betty had an excellent civilian position managing the U.S. Embassy liquor shop. Ginny attended an international school run by Dominican nuns. Because their home and lifestyle in Taiwan were well established, Aunt Betty and Ginny would continue to live there during Uncle Ed's tour in Viet Nam. They invited me to travel to Taiwan to keep Betty and Ginny company for the coming year while Ed would be away.

Being somewhat shy, not very adventurous, and committed to my fledgling banking career, I politely declined the invitation. Then Uncle Ed and my mother ganged up on me, convincing me that I was being offered the opportunity of a lifetime, and, if I didn't like it there, I could certainly return home to Massachusetts. Being a very compliant young lady, I acquiesced, although I had no personal desire to take this trip.

So began a year of priceless experiences that would open my eyes to a world far different from any I had ever known. During that year I would grow up, reaching a maturity level I would not have attained living at home with my parents. I would begin to define my true self.

About 12 hours into the 24 hour flight, I suddenly experienced a sort of revelation that began my metamorphosis from being the shy, serious, reticent person everybody perceived me to be, to the open and friendly, adventurous, self-confident person I wanted to be. It occurred to me that when I got off the plane, it would be like starting my life anew. I would be living and working in a whole new world, meeting all new people who had no preconceptions about me or my personality. Even Aunt Betty had not seen me in years and really didn't know me. I was free to become the woman I wanted to be.

My only point of reference for Chinese culture was Boston's Chinatown, so I had imagined Taiwan would be just a larger version. I could not have been more wrong! Visiting Chinatown was still visiting a part of Boston, Massachusetts, USA. Getting off that plane in Taipei was like landing on another planet. My senses were flooded with new sights, sounds, and smells. That first ride through the streets to my new home was quite overwhelming and frightening. The fetid smell from the open sewerage ditches nauseated me. As I observed romantic couples walking hand-in-hand beside the stinking polluted river, I thought they must have been crazy. I never would have believed that a few months from that night, I would be enjoying my own romantic stroll by that same visually beautiful river, and that I also would become oblivious to the stench!

When I alighted from the car in Aunt Betty's yard, one member of the house staff set off a seemingly endless string of firecrackers right behind me, causing me to jump and shriek. All the house staff applauded my panicked reaction. Aunt Betty explained this was a traditional welcome!

Though I was exhausted and jet-lagged, the following evening I was the guest of honor at an elaborate restaurant feast with many of my aunt's and uncle's Chinese and American military friends. After the restaurant manager's lengthy search produced a small fork stamped "U.S. Army" (obviously from a mess kit) for me, I was determined to make learning to use chopsticks my priority for the following day! However, for that night I was granted a "grace period." The food was wonderful and included a masterpiece Peking Roast Duck. I made a valiant effort to keep up appearances in spite of my jet-lagged state. Then, at the end of the feast, the chef came from the kitchen and proudly approached me with a platter. Clearly, I was being honored with some special delicacy. I looked down and was horrified to see a duck's head split open and its brain exposed! My aunt's Chinese friend instructed me to eat the brains because they would make me wise. He picked up a portion on chopsticks and held it in front of my mouth. I crumbled, completely dissolving into hysterical tears. Try as I might, I could not get a grip on myself. My aunt made profuse apologies for my embarrassing breach of dinner party etiquette and ushered me out to a waiting taxi. I sobbed all the way home but received no comfort from Aunt Betty. I went to bed still crying and fell asleep making mental plans to return to Massachusetts.

The following day I woke up, still very tired from jet lag, realizing at that point that I was too tired to face the return trip to the States right away. The thought of getting back on a plane for 24 hours completely devastated me. I knew I could not do it at that time, but I resolved to return to Massachusetts as soon as I felt rested enough.

While Betty was at work, I hung out in the house. After a while I went out in the yard taking in what I could see of the neighborhood, listening to the sounds, smelling the aromas, and trying to absorb the atmosphere. When Betty came home from work, we sat and talked. She was serious and somewhat stern, reminding me that I was now in another culture. *I* was the foreigner, and when in Rome, do as the Romans do. Or in this case, when in Taiwan, do as the Chinese! I apologized sincerely for my "transgression" of the previous evening. I told Aunt Betty I did not think my being in Taiwan would work out, but I was too exhausted for the return trip. I would like to stay a couple of weeks, get my feet under me, and then go home. Aunt Betty did not argue about my wish to return.

The next day, when Betty was at work, I decided to explore. I walked to the little Taiwanese village not far from our house, and I browsed around. When I got back to the house, our house maid was quite distraught because I had gone out of the yard. When I told her where I had been, she laughed. She could not believe it because my aunt had lived in that house for several years and not once had she ventured into that market area. (Given Betty's social station, she patronized upscale establishments in the city or on the base.)

Betty had given me some Taiwan currency, and the following day, I revisited the marketplace. I ended up having my hair done in a village beauty shop, which was quite an adventure for all concerned! The hairdresser called in all of his neighbors and family to watch, and he encouraged me to teach his children some English. My blond hair and blue eyes fascinated everyone! When Betty came home from work, she could not believe my hair. It looked fabulous and had cost me the equivalent of $.25 in US money! Betty, who normally went to a hairdresser in a fancy hotel, was so impressed at my hairdo, that she had me take her to the village hairdresser as well! For the rest of my time in Taiwan, the two of us always went to the village hairdresser.

During the next couple of weeks, I continued settling in and exploring. I went out on my own and secured a job teaching English conversation classes several hours a day to young military officers at an international language institute run by the Nationalist Chinese military. My aunt investigated Chinese language courses offered on base for Americans, and I enrolled in a beginner's course.

By the end of the two weeks I had set for the limit of my Taiwan stay, I felt such a comfort level that I knew I would *not* be going home. Neither Betty nor I broached the subject again and that was fine.

From that point on, I threw myself into the culture and discovered things that I never would have had the opportunity to experience otherwise. Most of my companions were Chinese and Taiwanese friends I had met at the schools or in the neighborhood. Almost all of them could read and write English, but had some difficulty conversing in the language. They appreciated the opportunity to practice speaking English with me, and reciprocally, I practiced speaking Mandarin Chinese with them. We had no problems communicating. We formed some wonderful friendships, keeping in touch for many years after I returned to the States.

I rode city buses all around Taipei for a fare of five cents. Friends and I traveled by train to more distant and rural territories where we hiked trails up mountainsides overlooking breathtaking views of rice paddy terraces and waterfalls. Unlike America, where public restrooms abound in retail establishments, plumbing and flush toilets were few and far between in Taiwan in those days. Oftentimes, a restroom was nothing more than a "squatter," meaning a hole in the floor. I quickly developed phenomenal bladder control so I could wait many hours until I returned from my excursions and could avail myself of the comfortable bathroom in our house with its clean porcelain flush toilet. (The control I learned to exercise then certainly has been a valuable asset all these years later now that I have ALS and am dependent on caregivers to take me to the bathroom!)

I saw temples filled with elaborate lanterns, gilded statues, and incense. Other cities had enormous statues of Buddha, larger than a building. Funerals sometimes passed along the streets, and to me they looked more like parades, with their loud music, marchers, and even "floats." The costumes, drama, and cacophony of sound that is Chinese opera mesmerized me. The performance of Chinese acrobats doing seemingly impossible feats before my eyes left me spellbound. I watched Chinese martial arts movies with five sets of subtitles on the screen, including English, in the attempt to cover most of the languages commonly spoken in Taiwan. (Although Mandarin Chinese was now the official national language, many people used other dialects and even the forbidden Japanese-Taiwanese language.) I attended a Chinese wedding ceremony held in a Catholic church where the solemn Mass was followed by loud strings of firecrackers set off right inside the church!

Touring an Oriental rug factory, I was shocked to see that most of the workers were children, some quite small. The employer actually housed, fed and educated them! A 15 year old girl left her task for a few minutes to talk with me in surprisingly good English. She shared with me that although she missed living at home with her family, she was very happy living, working and being educated at the rug factory. She matter-of-factly explained that if she had not been given this opportunity she would probably have had to become a prostitute! (That "profession" was legal.) She seemed to look at her situation as something like a work /study program, while to me, a young American woman, it seemed very near to slavery!

 I tasted foods and flavors that I never tasted before or since. My students took me on "field trips" to shop and haggle in alley markets in the city and to restaurants that were not four or five star glamorous hot spots. One day we were in an alleyway marketplace and we stopped to eat noodles at a wagon in the street. (You could equate it to a hot pretzel wagon in NYC.) One of the young men in my class said to me, "Miss Linda, you are not like other Americans. We could never take another American here. We can take you anywhere!" Apparently, they thought I was different because I was open to anything and everything. I would never turn up my nose at any suggestion of a place to visit or a restaurant at which to eat. I considered that young man's remark to be very complimentary.

I love to eat and try different foods – other than duck brains! Actually, there was just one other time I refused to try something. One day my group of students took me to a restaurant where the specialty was cobra! Much like our seafood restaurants, where there is an aquarium with lobsters or such swimming around and you choose the one you want, this restaurant had an aquarium with live cobra, and you picked your own! The cobra was considered a delicacy, and everyone at the table tried it, but I could not. The entire time we were dining, I felt as if reptiles were slithering over my feet. Of course it was my imagination. I think perhaps if cobra had been served to me already cooked, I would have tried it. Seeing the live cobra first, I just could not handle it mentally. For that dining experience, I became a vegetarian!

In addition to my many Chinese friends, I also had an American friend who was a few years younger than I. Sarah Jane was the daughter of American military colleagues of my aunt and uncle. We met and became close when she came to Taiwan for a vacation visit. She lived with her parents in Hong Kong, and later, I was able to visit her there for a few weeks. Hong Kong is without a doubt the most fascinating place I have ever been.

In addition to my Asian cultural adventures, living with Aunt Betty also involved me in many social activities associated with her U.S. embassy and military connections. Aunt Betty's Taiwanese "sew girl" designed and made a few cocktail dresses and a formal gown for me. At first I felt somewhat like Cinderella, but I soon grew confident and thoroughly enjoyed my experiences at the formal dinners, cocktail parties, and even my first ball. In America, I had never even gone to my high school prom!

During my year in Taiwan, one of my language students, Tommy Chang, and I became close friends. We had a great deal in common and we were very attracted to each other. Eventually that friendship developed into a romance. Tommy introduced me to his family. Tommy's father was a bank official, his brother an artist, and his sister a fashion model. His mother enjoyed her role of homemaker. Tommy's family was somewhat westernized, very educated, and appeared to be living in a comfortable economic bracket. The family welcomed me in their home and took me with them on several outings to places I would never have seen otherwise, greatly contributing to my overall experience in Taiwan.

One evening we were at a party and Tommy was reading palms. This is something he had done many times before. Everyone at the party approached him, so of course, I did, too. He took my hand and began reading my future. I don't remember the details, but his forecast was of a positive nature, like a successful career and a generally happy life. Suddenly he stopped and closed my hand. He was very distressed, and he said, "That's all." I countered with, "What do you mean, that's all? Continue." However, he refused, despite my repeated requests. Ultimately, he said, "Never mind. Don't worry. It's far, far away." He never would tell me what he had seen. Now I wonder if he possibly saw my illness in my future. For several days thereafter, I kept asking him to reveal my palm's secret, but he never would.

I realized our relationship had become quite serious when Tommy invited me to accompany him to meet his American godmother, an elderly woman Tommy called "Auntie". She was a missionary who had been in Mainland China during the revolution and had a personal connection to Madam Chiang Kai Chek. "Auntie" was greatly revered by Tommy's family. It was obvious that we visited her to seek her blessing and seal of approval.

As I prepared to return home after a year, Tommy indicated to me that he wanted to get married. When I got home, he sent me a ring and asked me to marry him. I accepted his proposal and we began to plan our future. However, as time went on, the situation became politically complicated. Tommy was moving up in the ranks of the Nationalist Army, and to marry him I would have had to relinquish my American citizenship and adopt Nationalist Chinese citizenship. Had I been able to retain a dual citizenship, I probably would have married Tommy and moved to Taiwan. However, I could not renounce my American citizenship. He understood. After a time, we amicably broke off the engagement. Eventually Tommy married and sent me photographs from his wedding.

I can now extend a belated thanks to my mother and uncle for pressuring me into going to live in Taiwan for a year and affording me some of the most rewarding experiences of my life. During that time of wonderful adventures, I matured and became much more self-confident. Most importantly, I learned a fundamental truth about human nature: underneath cultural and racial diversity, people are all essentially the same. We all get hungry, thirsty, and tired. We all feel pride and shame, anger and envy. We all experience happiness and joy, sadness and grief. And we all seek friendship and love.

Chapter 7
Accommodations

Linda:

I have always believed that with this disease my only hope has been to stay in the race. I am running a race I will not win, but I have tried to be a competitor. A very big part of that is being *proactive* rather than *reactive*. With ALS and the speed at which it progresses, the ability to do anything can be taken away overnight or even in the same day. I have had the experience where in the morning, I could turn on a light switch, and four hours later, I could no longer perform that same function. My ability to do it was lost forever. So, my policy has been to plan ahead and try to put a system in place that will carry me forward for awhile in daily living activities.

I began making little accommodations when I was still living in the townhouse condo. Taking my trash to the dumpster became a real problem. Traversing the front stairs, carrying the bags to the dumpster, opening the bins and lifting the covers to throw the trash in was hard work and becoming harder and harder every day. At first I would open my front door and throw the bags down the stairs. When they hit the bottom I would climb down the stairs and literally drag them to the dumpster. For awhile that was working. One day I was at the dumpster, struggling to lift the covers on the various recycle bins and then lift my bags of trash into the bins. There was a young man who was there with his son who was eight or nine. The father said to the boy, "Steve, please help that lady with her trash." So the little boy helped me, and I thanked the father, who was a neighbor, but not someone I knew in the complex. I commented to him about my struggling and my crutches, and the like, and the father told to me that his son could help me out regularly. We made arrangements for Steve to stop by my house 2-3 times a week after school and take my trash out for me. I offered to compensate him, but the father said it was not necessary.

A few days later my doorbell rang, and there was little Steve to take out my trash. I told him that I really appreciated it, and if he wanted the job on a regular basis, I would compensate him at $1/bag. This little boy lit up like a Christmas tree at my suggestion! He took out three bags, I gave him $3, and he was thrilled. Two or three days later he showed up again, and when I went to pay him, he said "No thank you." I told Steve that I did not want him to disobey his dad, but it was my trash and he was working for me, and I would like to pay him. Then I asked him to tell his dad to call me so we could discuss it. He took the money that day. His dad did not call me, but later that day, Steve came back with a big grin, and advised me that his dad had agreed. For the remainder of my residence there – at least several months – Steve continued to do that job for me. He would come in, go right to the trash, bundle it up, and take it away. He did a good job. He was very careful to put the recyclables in the right place all the time. It was kind of fun. We did not have a set day for pick up, but I always knew when he needed money because he would show up at the door and ask, "Do you have trash?" This was an accommodation that was facilitated very easily by a neighborhood child. I'll bet many disabled people probably have children living in their neighborhoods who could do similar chores that would be a big help. I don't know what Steve did for a living when I moved away!

~~~~~~~~~~~~~~~~~~~~~~~~~~

A Variety of Accommodations
One of the things I procured to help myself was a cutting board with an edge around it. You place a sandwich against the edge and draw a knife through it. The edge keeps the bread from moving and makes cutting it so much easier. This board has two nails sticking up through the surface. You can impale meat, fruit, or vegetables on the nails and that holds it for you while you slice. This cutting board was extremely helpful.

I created a lot of my own accommodations. It was very difficult for me to open the door on the clothes dryer. I discussed it with my physical therapist and we figured out that if we applied a handle to the exterior of the drier, like a lever that I could push down, then I could pop open the door. My friend Mike made such a lever and drilled it onto the door of the dryer. For months, I was able to continue operating that machine and opening the door. Opening the washing machine door was also a problem and I used a kitchen knife as a lever to lift the lid. An occupational therapist took some very thick, thick, wire and made a loop that I could hook on to the washer control to activate the machine.

There were a million other little things I devised. In my fridge, things would drift to the back, and I could not reach in and pull them out. I got some little wire racks and I laid them on their side against the back wall of the fridge, essentially keeping the things from sliding back. That eliminated half of my usable refrigeration space, but that was not an issue. This accommodation made it possible for me to use the fridge.

Campbells' makes something called "Soup at Hand," which is in a sipable cup. I was watching TV and saw a commercial for it. Soup was impossible for me to feed myself. I thought, "I could put a straw in that sipable cup and just sip soup through a straw." At that time I was still able to hold a cup, so this was another useful adaptation.

In order to carry something from one place to another, I started hooking a very lightweight wicker basket over my arm when I first walked with crutches. Later, I put it over the walker.

When I was first diagnosed, my sister suggested I get an adjustable bed – not a hospital bed – with back raises and foot raises. That bed has been critical, especially more recently because at night breathing is a real issue. It can be adjusted to help alleviate congestion.

In the kitchen there were countless little modifications. I used easy-grip kitchen tools. Instead of the pop-up wipes for the counter, I found a brand that had wipes in a flat bin. I could open the bin and pull out a wipe. The pop ups created too much resistance. I could not pull them out. I learned how to put a glass drink bottle like V8 or iced tea on its side on the counter on a piece of sticky rubber, hold it down with one hand and manage to twist the cap off with the other. Usually I would spill a portion, but I got it open. I moved countless things for easier access. On all my drawer handles, the occupational therapist made wire loops that I could hook a finger into and just pull to open. There were so many little accommodations utilized daily that made it possible for me to function. One time when a new occupational therapist came out here thinking that she was going to change my life with all her handy dandy ideas, she ended up taking notes from me, and said to me, "You have the heart and soul of an occupational therapist."

One of the major accommodations involved cutting out the side of my fiberglass tub, essentially creating a walk-in shower. That was quite costly – about $800. An occupational therapist had given me the idea. She said that in some elderly housing units she had been working in, she had seen tubs that had been converted to a walk-in shower. She had no idea how it was done. I called a friend who was a plumber, thinking he might have info. He had never heard of it, but he knew someone who was a fiberglass expert, and we called that company. They knew immediately what I wanted, and they were able to accomplish it. At the time, I was still bathing myself. Even with the bars on the wall in the tub area, I had started falling. I had several major and embarrassing falls because I fell naked and wet getting out of the shower and I had to call for help to get back up. This accommodation enabled me to utilize the tub as a walk in shower, which made it much safer for me. Even though I presently have special shower equipment, that cut-out makes it easier. That was a very major accommodation.

(*Now you see print ads and commercials on TV all the time for this kind of tub cutaway that makes it much safer for elderly and disabled people to bathe. However, when Linda was in need of such a tub, very few people, including those in the industry, knew such a thing existed.*)

I repeatedly rearranged cupboards, shelves, closets, and drawers for more convenient access as my disease progressed. A regular toothbrush gave way to a power toothbrush. Toothpaste in a tube gave way to toothpaste in a pump, so I could just push down on it. I used writing utensils with easy grippers. Toilet paper was replaced by moist wipes, which were easier to handle. Even my wardrobe changed to clothing which required no fastening, such as pull-on bras (sports type), elastic waist pants and skirts, knee highs which replaced pantyhose, capes replaced coats and jackets. Long chains, which would slip over my head, took the place of shorter, clasp necklaces, and fish hook earrings replaced studs. Where there is a will, there is a way!

One evening as I was undressing to get ready for bed, I found that I could not pull my sweater off over my head. That same sweater had slid over my head so easily that morning. I tried repeatedly to pull it off, and I was working up a sweat and becoming physically exhausted. After about 45 minutes of fruitless effort, I was still trapped in my clothing with one arm in a sleeve, one arm out, and the turtleneck over my chin and mouth. In desperation, I telephoned a friend who was working nights at a nearby department store. She assured me she would come to rescue me in about 1-1/2 hours when she got off her shift. I sat down to wait. After about a half hour rest, I decided to give it one last attempt. With every bit of strength I could muster, I was able to pull off the sweater. I was so frustrated and elated at the same time that I sat on my bed laughing and crying for a few moments. When I had gained my composure, I called my friend and canceled the emergency visit. The following day I called another friend, Betsy, who was about my size. She came over and we combed through my closet removing several sweaters of the same offensive style, which Betsy then inherited.

When a regular iron became too heavy for me to use, I got a lightweight travel/steam iron. I replaced a regular ironing board with a small counter top ironing board. My new vacuum cleaner was now a lightweight electric broom. For quite awhile, I could always find an alternative if I just gave it some thought.

Somehow, I was able to find a solution for so many things that became problematic over time. There were a multitude of little everyday things that worked for awhile - things as simple as the touch lamp for my bedroom. I could not do a switch, but for a long time I could turn the light on and off just by touching it. My advice to any disabled person is: Don't let an obstacle that gets in your way make you think, "I can't do it." Find another way. Oftentimes there *is* another way. Presently, I am using someone else's hands, but for a long time I was able to do for myself because I made accommodations and found alternative ways. Being proactive means being resourceful.

Chapter 8
On the Job With ALS

Linda:

When I was quite clear about all the ramifications of my illness, I talked to my boss at the bank and told him what I was dealing with. He talked to his boss and the president of the bank. The president of the bank came up to my desk shortly thereafter, put an arm around my shoulder and said the bank was supporting me. As long as I was able to work and they needed me, the bank would try to make any accommodation necessary. They were wonderful.

My office was on the second floor. One of the first things they did was give me a reserved parking space near the back door and a key – my own private entrance. This saved me a long walk from the regular entrance. The building was pre-handicap regulations. There was some chit chat about putting a stair lift on the front stairs to get me to the second floor, but it was not realistic.

As the disease progressed, I was still working on the second floor, but the back stairway had become very difficult for me to negotiate. I had a couple of falls. One night I worked late after everyone else had left. I fell on the stairs and I could not get back to my feet. Usually if I fell on the floor I needed someone else to help me get back up. If I fell on the stairs, I could use the railing to help get me up, but it was just too difficult this time. I remember trying to will myself to be calm because I knew panic wouldn't help. Ultimately I was able to get up, after about 10-15 minutes. I was using a Swedish crutch (*metal/aluminum crutch that fit around the wrist with handle for the hand – often used by those with cerebral palsy*) at this time, and when I finally got out to the parking lot, I was soaking wet with sweat, and it was very cold outside. It was after this episode that I made arrangements to be driven to and from work by co-workers. I paid them for gas.

Now that I was being driven to work, I entered the bank through the front door, but eventually I fell down those stairs as well. Once I fell in the rest room and had to scream for help. Falls were becoming more frequent. With ALS falls, there is no warning. One minute you're on your feet, the next minute you wipe out. As such, work was becoming more hazardous.

~~~~~~~~~~~~~~~~~~~~~~~

Leading Up to the End of Work

When to stop working was a big decision. It was also an economic decision and an insurance decision. I had been looking into Social Security disability income, and at that time, I could get on disability income, but I would be uninsured because the law says when someone goes on Social Security disability, there is a 24 month waiting period for Medicare health insurance. All of these things were troubling, and trying to figure out when I should leave work was a major decision. My doctors were advising me to stop working (This was around '99-'00). However, I felt that working was beneficial to my emotional well-being, and it was providing for my economic security at the time.

~~~~~~~~~~~~~~~~~~~~~~~

Through the ALS association, I was advised to get home care from the local Visiting Nurses Association (VNA), which was not easy to get. The VNA's policy is "If you are working, we cannot help you." I was still working at that time.

I realized that things were getting too difficult for me to continue working much longer. I did cut my hours way back. I was getting up at 5:30 in the morning to shower and dress to be picked up at 8:30. It took me 3 hours to get myself ready for work, and I was reducing my hours in the office. I had several falls at work, and I could see the writing on the wall. However, I was waiting for a sign to tell me when to stop. On December 26, 2000, I had scheduled an appointment with the VNA physical therapist to come to my home for an evaluation. That morning my friend Fran came to pick me up to take me to work. As we walked toward her car, I was struggling every step of the way. It seemed like a mile for what was probably 25 yards. Fran said to me, "You know you cannot keep doing this." I responded that I knew, but just did not know how or when to stop. Today was today and that was all that mattered, and I could do it today. She dropped me off at the office.

By this time I had been relocated to a branch office entirely on the ground floor, and they made accommodations for me there. They put up bars by the door that I could grasp and pull myself up the one step to get into the office. As I tried to step up that one step, I fell. Tom, the office manager, was there. He came over, helped me to my feet and said, "I'll help you in." We tried again with him attempting to give me a boost. I could not get up that stair. Ultimately, after several attempts, I was weak and shivering from overwhelming fatigue resulting from my repeated efforts. I knew I could not do it. Tom and a friend's husband, who happened to stop in the office right at that time, drove me home. Fran brought my push wheelchair out and the men got me in the wheelchair and lifted me up the outside three stairs and into my house. I knew right then and there that the sign had come. I could not continue to work.

That afternoon I sat in my condo. Fran stayed with me for awhile. Ultimately, I was able to get to my feet and use my crutches to get to the bathroom, and then I sat back down in the living room. Fran left and I was waiting for that physical therapist who showed up later that afternoon. I told him that everything had changed that very morning and that I did not believe I could safely return to work. His evaluation went forward on the basis of my being homebound.

My company was terrific. Before this happened, they had already put the wheels in motion for their long term disability compensation program under their insurance. I was able to start collecting a portion of my pay. My "retirement" was now official, as of the end of December, 2000.

Chapter 9
Home Health Care

From the outset of Linda's diagnosis, she was determined to be as independent as possible, for a long as possible. She would be the first to tell you she was a "control freak," and she had every intention of being in control of her own life as long as she was physically and mentally capable.

Ever since her divorce many years before she contracted ALS, Linda had lived alone. Early on in her disease, I remember commenting to her that it was too bad that she wasn't married and had someone who could help with her care through this disease. She immediately said to me that it was much better for her to be alone in this situation because in order to fight the disease, she had to be single-minded and self-centered which is not conducive to a good marital relationship. By nature, Linda was the antithesis of the egotistical and self-absorbed personality. However, with self-preservation at stake, she was able to switch gears, keep the focus on her needs, and become her own best advocate. It might not have worked for everyone, but Linda could do anything she set her mind to.

Once Linda stopped working, almost everything changed drastically. Through the Visiting Nurse's Association, she began weekly physical therapy sessions with John Matson, who became her regular physical therapist. Also, she was able to get some assistance at home for a few hours a day. That assistance was critical, as it was becoming increasing difficult for her to manage many of her needs.

At this stage she needed assistance with bathing, dressing, and food preparation, as well as help with light housekeeping and laundry. The several hours a day that the VNA provided for Linda in home assistance was not adequate for her needs. So Linda hired some friends to do things like get her up in the morning and put her to bed at night.

This arrangement worked out well for awhile, but as her illness progressed, she realized that her friends were not capable of handling her increasing disabilities. She had to hire health care workers who had more experience working with disabled patients. Linda was usually able to find such workers through word-of-mouth, friends of friends, etc. who were looking to pick up a few extra bucks working under the table. Linda eventually hooked up with other home care services to acquire more assistance when it became necessary.

Even at this point, most people in Linda's situation would have thrown in the towel and moved into a nursing home, where they would get plenty of skilled care 24/7. That was unthinkable to Linda! She was adamant about avoiding a nursing home at all costs. To her, a nursing home was tantamount to digging her own grave and jumping in. Independence was everything, and if that meant having a constant flow of health care workers parading though her condo each day to take care of her, then that was the way to go.

Chapter 10
Falling

Linda:

Falling is part of ALS. When you are still able to stand and walk, you will fall all of a sudden for no reason. One minute you are standing, the next second you are lying on the floor. There is no warning. Everyone thinks that you are tripping, that it's the rug, that it's this or that. In fact, it's ALS, and you fall for no reason at all. People laugh at the joke, "I've fallen and I can't get up." Well, when it's happening for real, it's not funny at all. For me, falling was a big psychological blow. Whenever I would fall and need assistance to get up, I felt incompetent, and it would depress me. I felt very unworthy. I don't know why. It took me a long time to finally realize that it *was not* my fault, and I did not need to feel guilty when I fell.

When I would fall at work, co-workers would pick me up. A couple of times when I fell at work they would phone the fire department, which is an excellent thing to do. When a person falls, if they are unable to get up, trying to drag them to their feet is not recommended. You can not only hurt them, but you can hurt yourself. Firefighters help with this all the time. Two big strong men, one on each side of you and boom – you're on your feet again!

Someone I worked with recommended the "Lifeline" system, and I obtained that. I wear a button, and if I fall and I can't get up, I hit the button and a loudspeaker on my phone is activated to the Lifeline Company. They ask me what I need and I tell them I fell, and I am uninjured, but I need firemen to get me on my feet. The Lifeline company immediately accesses the fire department, and they are here within minutes.

I have fallen well over 100 times. I have been blessed with and thankful for the extra weight I carry because I truly believe a thinner person would have broken a hip. The worst week I ever had, I fell 11 times in an eight day period. By the time that week was over I was physically and emotionally beaten up, but my bones remained intact!

Because a friend of mine is a firefighter, I became aware of a valuable item called the *KNOX-BOX*. You give the fire department a key to your home. They put it in a locked box by your front door. They have the key to this box. They come to your home, open the box, remove your key, and open your door with it. No one – no social worker or anybody else I talked to - knew anything about this. The fire department orders the box for you (about $60), and they install it for you. Then they can always get into your house. Interestingly, one of the firemen in town commented to me, "Too bad more disabled and elderly people in town do not have these." In this town, I am one of two people who have a KNOX-BOX. I told him that more people would have them if they were aware of the service, but it is one of those well kept secrets.

I had an electronic door opener installed previous to the installation of the KNOX-BOX. I wore the remote for it all the time, so there was never an instance when the firemen could not get into my house after I had fallen. It did happen once in Abington before I moved here. They came and were locked out. They wanted to smash my door in, but I yelled to them to wait because I called a friend who had a key. I knew she was coming over to let them in.

The worst and the most frightening fall I had happened in my bedroom one morning when my helper was in the kitchen getting me tea. I was transferring from my wheelchair to the walker. I lost my balance and crashed to the floor, smashing into my mirror-paneled closet doors. Cathy, my helper, heard the crash, and came rushing in to find me on the floor, covered with broken glass. That was tricky. We called the fire department. They came out, got me to my feet, and put me in my wheelchair, still covered with glass. Cathy had to leave and go to work. I called my health aide who was scheduled to come, to warn her of what had happened in case she wanted to bring a back up. She came out by herself and I still don't know how she did it. She got me out of my nightclothes, into the shower, and managed to wash all that glass out of my hair and off my skin without getting cut herself. I had just a few pinpricks. That was quite an incident.

As far as falls go, if anyone is in a position of falling, you definitely need a lifeline phone rescue support system and you definitely need a way for help to get into your home. The electric door lock and the fire department KNOX-BOX are essentials, as far as I am concerned. More people need to be aware of these things.

Chapter 11
Soul Sisters

Linda had a wide circle of friends. However, Patty was always her closest friend and soul mate. When I interviewed Patty, she not only covered how she and Linda first met, but she touched on so many other aspects of their lives through the years. Initially, I was going to include only a small portion of Patty's narrative, as it is far longer than I had envisioned for this project. However, Patty enlightens us with so many varied snapshots of Linda's personality, that I decided to preserve its full scope. It is a look at Linda through the eyes of the person who knew her best. Because of its length, Patty's recollections of their experiences as adults will be featured in another chapter.

Here are some reminiscences of two best friends who have very different accounts of their first meeting.

Linda:

Patty insists that we met in the 8th grade. I think it was the 7th grade! I remember we had a music class together and also homeroom. Every day Patty would say hi to me. I, being a very shy person, never answered her.

One day, she finally stopped by my desk in homeroom and said, "Why don't you ever answer me? I say hi to you every day." I had no reply for her. However, after that we became best friends.

It was a match made in heaven, because she had six siblings at home, while I had none, as my sister had long since moved out when she got married. So for me, playing and visiting at Patty's house was wonderful with all those kids around. For her, playing and visiting at my house was wonderful because there were no other kids around.

Patty had an old player piano in her cellar with hundreds and hundreds of music rolls for the piano. I would go to her house after school or on a weekend and she and I would spend hours at that piano playing the music and singing along to those old, old songs. We loved it.

We hung out at my house in the summer because we had a little above ground swimming pool, and she enjoyed that. The rest of the time we hung out at her house, amusing ourselves with the player piano. To me, growing up as a virtual only child from the time I was ten (when my sister got married), the commotion at Patty's house was fun. Her mother could not have cared less about having another kid around.

We were on the same academic level in our classes in junior high. We had classes together and she and I commiserated over our problems and helped each other with our homework. We were both very studious. As we entered high school, we did not see as much of each other because she was in the college prep program and I was in the business program. We remained close friends, even though we did not see each other as much in school.

Patty worked at the Brockton Public library – the Montello branch. I worked at the Gas Company, and we really did not do anything out of the ordinary. We never had any *big* adventures together. It has been a "quiet friendship." Once she and I went to Hyannis, I think by bus. I remember I took her into Boston once when we were in the 9th grade. She had never been there before. We went shopping and had lunch. THAT was a big adventure!

When we both were in different colleges, we still got together a lot. I often went to plays or some of the sporting events at Stonehill (where she went to college) with her. Occasionally we would go to a concert. I believe we went to some folk music concerts – Judy Collins and Gordon Lightfoot are just two examples. There has never been any real distance between us, even though our lives were on different paths.

Patty met Garry at Stonehill. He was a very possessive boyfriend. He did not want her to have time for anyone but him. He thought all her time should be spent with him. She used to spend time with me without him knowing. Nothing, not even Garry, was going to come between our friendship! At first, I am sure Garry saw me as someone who was compromising Patty's attention, and he did not like that. Patty, on the other hand, didn't care because she never stopped seeing me as a friend.

I think the first time I met Garry, the three of us went to a play at Stonehill. At the time, I thought Patty and Garry were very different. Garry is quiet and kind of brooding, while Patty is outgoing and cheerful. They got married while I was in Taiwan, and they have been together for almost 40 years, so it obviously works.

When Jim Burge and I got married, the four of us socialized together. Garry and Jim got along quite well – both were cynical, looked on the dark side of things, and loved to debate an issue – any issue, for the purpose of the debate. As two couples, we did a lot together, and we enjoyed a good friendship.

When Patty's sister was found dead, she turned to me. Jim and I went over to her house after the wake, and we hung out there for hours that night with Pat and Garry. We talked, and talked. When we were leaving, Garry hugged me and said that he wanted to thank me very much for being with Pat at the time. He felt my presence had helped her through that difficult period. At that instant, I felt the barrier disappearing from Garry.

I remember when we were visiting them for dinner once and Garry invited Jim to go into their basement playroom for video games or whatever it was. Garry said something to the effect that they might as well retire to the other room because when Patty and I were together there was no room for men anyway! The four of us attended some concerts, shows, movies, etc.

Patty and I have a true friendship. We have never had to explain anything to each other. We have always been there for each other – through thick and thin. Garry, not long ago, gave me a very nice compliment. I e-mailed to thank him for some assistance he'd given me. He e-mailed back that he was always happy to help. He said that Patty, being who she is, has many, many friends. To him, they are just that – his wife's friends. But I am also *his* friend. It made me cry.

Two important elements playing a key role in the friendship between Patty and myself have been music and books. We've always enjoyed the same music and the same books. If she loans me a book and says she loved it, I know I will as well. A few weeks ago I told her about a book I was reading called *My Sister's Keeper*. She went to the library, borrowed it, and loved it so much she recommended it to her book club!

The friendship has endured over 45 years. In all the time of our friendship, we have never, ever had one argument, which is quite amazing – especially when you consider how easy it is for teenaged girls to fight. I have been blessed with wonderful friends.

~~~~~~~~~~~~~~~~~~~~~~~~~~~~

Patty:
As I recollect, Linda and I met at the end of seventh grade at North Junior High School in Brockton. We were in the same homeroom. At that time, on the last day of school, you would go to your new homeroom so you would be able to find it on the first day of school in September. When I got to this homeroom, I looked around and I didn't know anybody at all. I recognized Linda. Though we had not been together in seventh grade, I somehow knew who she was, and that she was going to be in all my classes the next year.

When we had a chance, I introduced myself to her, and I said, "I think we are going to be in the same classes next year." She responded positively and that was the beginning of what became a most enduring friendship.

Then the next year, being in the same homeroom and having all our classes together, we became friendly, and started exchanging visits to each other's houses. I think one of the things that attracted us to each other was that we came from such different backgrounds. I am the oldest in a family of seven children, and Linda was the younger of only two children. At that point her sister had married and moved away from home, so Linda was like an only child. She loved coming to my house with all of the noise and commotion, and eating at a huge table with my family. We would go down to the cellar and have fun with the player piano, singing all the old-fashioned songs. We would share a twin-sized bed when she stayed for sleepovers. She always seemed to enjoy my family, which was nice for me because sometimes one can get overwhelmed with a family that size. I loved going to her house because it was quiet and peaceful and we were left alone to do whatever we wanted. I would also go up to NH with her and visit her family at their camp. That was fun for me because we didn't do anything like that in my family. I think our relationship was almost like a marriage because we brought different things to it along with different backgrounds.

When Linda came to my house, she thought my parents didn't notice that there was another child around. That wasn't quite true because there weren't that many people who were invited to have dinner with us or to stay overnight. Linda was an exception. My parents always liked having her. When we went to the swimming pool, she would just pile into the car with the rest of us. She was accepted like one of the family. That was unusual for my parents who did not like all of our friends.

At that time, Linda was one of the bravest and most daring people I knew. We would go into Boston by ourselves on the bus and spend the day. I would no sooner have thought of doing that in my little existence in Brockton than going to the moon. My family didn't go into Boston. We didn't go to many places. With that many children, it was too difficult to go out to eat or do much of anything. We did go to the zoo, parks, and places like that, but we didn't go into the city at all. So going into Boston with Linda was a real adventure. We went Christmas shopping and I was able to get things for my family that I wouldn't have been able to get otherwise. We went to Bailey's for sundaes. Linda had the whole day planned out and I just kind of went along. Linda was always the leader and I was the follower. She just seemed to know what to do. She was much savvier and had more world knowledge than I had. Part of it was because she was born in Medford and had gone into the city (Boston) a lot with her parents, so she was more familiar with it.

Linda gave me the first surprise birthday party I ever had. I think we were in ninth grade and I was 14. She had planned the party which was held at her house. Her mother made a marble cake decorated with buttercream frosting. We had a scavenger hunt, where you had to go around the neighborhood and find different objects. That was our entertainment. She had asked some of my friends and some of our common friends – about ten people altogether. It was a wonderful day, and the first time I ever had a surprise party, or even a party with just friends.

In the eighth grade, our class was going to put on Gilbert and Sullivan's *HMS Pinafore*. Linda said she and I should try out for it. I agreed. We both auditioned, singing alone. I got accepted. Linda didn't. I felt badly for Linda, especially since the whole thing was her idea! However, it did not hurt our friendship.

In eighth grade music class we were required to get up and perform something in front of the class. We were all dreading it. You could do it alone or with others. Linda suggested we get together and do something as a group. Fine with me! Another friend, Kathy, joined us, and the three of us were going to do a song from Rodgers and Hammerstein's *Flower Drum Song*. It was something about understanding the other generation. We went to Linda's house and practiced the whole thing. The day came for us to perform it and Linda was absent! I was so mad because Kathy and I had to get up by ourselves and do the song. That was one time that I was angry with Linda. I am sure, however, that I did not yell at her. When I spoke to her on the phone I said, "How come you weren't in school today?" She said she had a stomach ache. I just let it alone, but I was not a happy camper with her.

Linda was competitive, and we did compete for grades, though it never came between our friendship. I remember in algebra, for some reason I got better grades than she did. Don't ask me how. She got Bs and I got As, but she was always trying to get that A. I may have been an algebra person, but it was Linda who ended up in the business world, so obviously she had math smarts. Our competition was always friendly. Though Linda was very competitive, I don't think I was quite as competitive, or felt I had to win all the time. I was just very conscientious. I look at myself as a plugger. I would spend as long as it took to get the problem right. It wasn't because I wanted to be the best. It's just been my nature my entire life. I always spend as long as it takes to get something done.

Linda and I both liked to write, and when we were in the ninth grade there was a contest sponsored by the Brockton Enterprise, the local newspaper. The contest was in honor of George Washington's birthday, and you had to write about what George Washington might do in the present time – the early 60s - to solve some of the world's problems. We both entered the contest. Part of Linda's essay was published in the paper because one of the judges was a columnist for the paper, and he mentioned how impressed he was with her writing. Mine was NOT mentioned, and for the first time, I was a little jealous of her! I do not remember what I wrote, but mine was a letter to George Washington. As it turned out, I won first prize! My friend, Linda, won second prize! We were both very happy. First prize was an Easter outfit, and second prize was a watch. Linda wanted the watch, so she was thrilled. Fortunately, this competition did not affect our friendship at all.

The main job Linda had throughout junior high and high school was babysitting. She enjoyed children very much and was in great demand. She kindly recommended me as a back-up for those she could not accommodate. Even when she came to my house as a teen-ager, she was always interested in my younger siblings, what they were doing, and what they wanted to do in the future. I think *she* talked to them more than I did. In later years, when her friends had children of their own, these children were often included in her plans. I remember she and Jim hosting a cook-out at their home for several couples with youngsters. When the Circus was in town, she even invited my children to go as her guests without their parents. This interest in young people continued throughout Linda's life. She respected and related to them extremely well. She would often recall anecdotes about her friends' children that even their parents had forgotten!

When we went to high school, we were in totally different sections starting from the tenth grade. I was in the college course and she was in the business course. We never saw each other in school because we had totally different classes and schedules. Yet somehow, we still kept going over each other's houses and doing things together. I lost some of my other friends whom I no longer saw. Looking back, it's surprising that Linda and I did stay together because our paths diverged quite drastically.

After high school, Linda went to Bryant and Stratton, a business school in Boston, for a year or two, and I went to Stonehill, a four-year college in Easton, but we still would get together. We also talked a lot on the phone. Even then, Linda was kind of an insomniac and she went to bed very late. She would stay up listening to talk radio, which I never did. She was a real night owl.

I was invited to Linda's graduation from Bryant and Stratton. I remember we were at her house and she was getting dressed. For some reason, she had a crying fit and she didn't want to go. Linda could be shy and nervous about public events at that time. Her mother had to talk to her. I didn't know what to do. I couldn't figure out what her problem was. I guess she felt that she didn't look nice, or that her dress wasn't good enough. She was upset about how she appeared. Linda was sensitive about that because she was a bit overweight going through junior high and high school. It took Linda's mom about a half hour to calm her down and convince her to go, however Linda was subdued for most of the day. It seems she had self-esteem issues about appearing in public. She was afraid of being the center of attention and not measuring up.

After Bryant and Stratton, Linda went to Taiwan for a year. Going to Taiwan was one of the best things that ever happened to her. She was on her own and was her own person.

We didn't communicate that much then. I got married to Garry, and she was not home at the time, but her parents came to my wedding. When she got back from Taiwan, she shared an apartment with her good friend Betsy until her marriage.

Chapter 12
From Walking to Wheelchair

Linda:

In my case, the progression of this disease has been slow, but it has been very steady as well. In the course of one day you can lose the ability to do something. Every day I have had some kind of loss. One of my doctors put it in the perspective of a pie. If you have a whole pie and cut a slice, there are still seven more slices, so it's no big deal, and not much of the pie is gone. As you keep chipping away at that pie, each successive piece you remove has a bigger impact on what is left. With your body, it is the same way. In the beginning, little losses make no big impact. You can accommodate, and you can learn to use another part of your body to make up for the loss. As the losses continue, less and less is there to compensate.

The way ALS attacked my body in the beginning I felt like a big *Stop Smoking* sign with a diagonal line across it. My weakness was my left arm and shoulder – across my body to my right leg and foot. It was like a diagonal line.

At the outset, I was walking with difficulty, but I was walking unassisted. After awhile it became very difficult, so I acquired a cane, and that gave me the support I needed. As time went on the cane was no longer adequate, so I got crutches. (I only used one crutch - the Swedish crutch - because one side of me was weaker than the other.) Time went on and I progressed to a walker. I went from a regular walker to a walker with wheels. All of these accommodations kept me going at work and at home.

Ultimately, I knew I would need a wheelchair. I did acquire a push wheelchair that I used just for outings at first. When it got to the point that I could no longer walk safely outside of my home, good friends took me to the beach, restaurants, the theater, and other such places, and they would push me around in my collapsible wheelchair. It made these outings possible for me.

However, my need for the fulltime wheelchair was increasing. I was diagnosed in January of '99. By August of '02 it was a necessity. In March of '03 I began thinking about power wheelchairs. I had gone on the internet and looked up some information, but I honestly had no idea of how to begin. One day my physical therapist John was here and I knew it was obvious to him that the time was drawing near for me to get a power wheelchair. I also realized that John, knowing me, was probably hesitant to broach the topic. He did not know that I had been doing some wheelchair research. That afternoon in March, he told me he had just been with a patient who had a new wheelchair that was quite nifty. I took the cue and I said to him, "I know I need to look into power wheelchairs and I have been doing some internet research but it's quite overwhelming." John said that he could call a vendor and they would have someone out here within a week. I agreed, so John placed a call to a company in Fall River, and in a day or two, a company rep was here.

The salesman who came out had a power wheelchair with him that was ready to be sold to me, and did not require pre-approval by Medicare because of the price. The problem was that it was not the wheelchair I needed then or would need in the future. It simply was not suitable. The salesman came in, running off at the mouth about this chair and how I could have it in a week. He talked about all the features and everything on it. He sat me in it. I knew it was not right for me. I was sitting there getting more and more annoyed as he extolled the virtues of that particular chair. Finally, he took a breath and John said, "Okay, that's great. Now let's discuss a chair that will suit Linda's needs." The sales rep was taken aback. John knew about my needs and about wheelchair evaluation, so he started to outline my requirements. The sales rep said to him, "Oh, well that will all have to be pre-approved by Linda's Medicare. It will take time, and they will probably reject it and we'll have to try again." He could see his instant commission being put on delay. John said, "Fine. We have time. She is not in critical need yet. I will write the evaluation, and we'll get it started." When John started writing up his assessment of my needs, the salesman told him to, "Make it a good story. You've got to make it sound good." John looked at him and said, "It's not a story. It's the truth."

The order was submitted, and it did take until August, but there were no delays or rejections. It all went forward without a hitch. I felt very grateful that John knew how to handle the salesman and knew the particulars about wheelchairs. He also understood what I needed. One of the features that I never would have thought of was the automatic recline. I use that all the time. When the chair was ordered, lateral supports were not a critical issue. I still had trunk stability. Now, without those, I could not sit. Basically, every part of the wheelchair is custom built. They measured me all over from the back of my butt to the kneecap, from kneecap to ankle, from ankle to foot, from shoulder to elbow, elbow to wrist. I would say if anyone is ever in the position of needing specialized assistive equipment, you should avoid dealing solely with a vendor. You need a therapist who is familiar with what is available and who knows what your particular needs are. It is also important to consider what your future needs will be. John made sure that as my disabilities progressed, adaptations could be made to the wheelchair.

At the time of this interview, Linda was in the process of adding adaptations to her wheelchair.

However I will add that the wheelchair expert at Spaulding who is working to make new adaptations to my wheelchair at the moment, did feel that we would have been better off if we had ordered from the beginning what I am going to end up with after the adaptations. I think I agree with her, but in John's defense, he probably never anticipated my being independent this long. He thought the chair we ordered would take me through. For me, the way my body is deteriorating, these adaptations are the end of the line. Some people, like Chris Reeve, have a puff control. I tried it with a computer mouse and I could not do it. So I think we have pretty much exhausted what we can do for me with wheelchair adaptations.

61

Cost – the first collapsible wheelchair – Blue Cross paid for it. The power wheelchair – 80% was paid by Medicare, and Blue Cross paid the other 20%. That chair cost $17,000. The head control I recently attached cost $9,000, and I have no idea about the automatic leg lifts and the new seating program. Medicare and Blue Cross will take care of it. The costs for this equipment are outrageously expensive.

Chapter 13
Tea Parties

Like me, Linda had a May birthday. Since my husband Norm's birthday was the last day of April, it had become a longstanding tradition for the three of us to get together and go out to eat in celebration of all three birthdays. When Linda was no longer capable of doing that, I still wanted to do something special for her birthday – special enough so that it would be her birthday present as well. But what? It finally hit me. Linda loved going to "afternoon tea," something she could no longer enjoy. So I decided that I would create a fancy shmancy high tea for her in her condo. When I called to propose the idea, she absolutely LOVED it!

Little did I realize what I was getting myself into. I had never done anything like this (a tea) before, and found out that it was an incredible amount of work (because I made everything from scratch). However, it was well worth it.

Once Linda agreed, we decided that she should invite three friends to come as guests. She picked out a date (Saturday, May 26, 2001), and I sent out invitations. I spent a lot of time going over menu options and presenting them to Linda. Linda was a lemon freak, so the one thing I knew I had to have was some kind of lemon dessert. Other than that, Linda was open to anything else on the menu.

We settled on a soup - butternut squash/sweet potato soup; a tea bread – lemon tea bread; three kinds of scones – nutty scones, orange chocolate chip, and triple chocolate; Devonshire cream, lemon curd, jam; four different kinds of tea sandwiches – English cucumber on wheat, curried egg on marble rye, chicken cashew on multi-grain, pinwheel roasted pepper on sun-dried tomato bread; a lemon dessert – lemon soufflé with raspberry sauce; "tuxedo" strawberries; and about five different varieties of loose teas. I made

63

up a special keepsake menu for everyone that opened like a book. Inside there was information about the history of afternoon tea and the appropriate "tea etiquette."

On the celebration day, I came early to Linda's to set up everything. We used her special fancy table linens, and picked from Linda's great variety of dinnerware. With a floral centerpiece, the table setting looked quite lovely.

Linda had invited three very good friends – Patty, Betsy, and Gail. Gail was nice enough to bring her three-tiered plate stand that I could use for most of the food. I collect tea pots, and I brought a couple of them over for the tea to add to the ones Linda had.

It was a delightfully festive tea party, and no one enjoyed it more than Linda. At the end, she was getting emotional (which rarely happened), talking about how much the party meant to her and how special it was for her to have her closest friends there, especially since it could be her last birthday celebration. At that point, we needed some levity, so I immediately said. "Linda, don't be crazy. I just started a tradition here. I am sure that for years to come, we are all going to be sitting right back here celebrating your birthday with tea party after tea party." Everyone chuckled and agreed… and that is exactly what happened! Every year after that, I made a special tea party for Linda's birthday. A few guests repeated, but she usually tried to invite different people each time. It was always a wonderful day for Linda, and I was truly grateful that I could do something each year that meant so much to her.

A week after the (first) tea party, Linda sent me the following letter:

June 2, 2001

Dear Leslie,

There are no words adequate for me to thank you for the extraordinary birthday tea party you gave me. Only you, Norm, and I know the tremendous amount of time and effort that you put into it. That you would do this for me touches me at the very bottom of my heart. Everything was perfect! The table looked so pretty, just like a Victorian tea room. And all of the exquisite food! I don't know what I thought was the most delicious. It is almost impossible for me to choose my favorites from the menu. I feasted on leftovers for the next few days. Everything tasted just as good after resting for awhile in my refrigerator! If forced to choose favorites from the menu, I guess my personal choices would be the soup, lemon bread with lemon curd, chicken salad, and the cream cheese/roasted pepper pinwheel. But those choices are only winners by a fraction, because everything was absolutely scrumptious. And your presentation was phenomenal! I called my sister that evening to tell her all about the party, and I told her that if I died that night I would die happy! Thank you, thank you for this most special birthday present, and for all the wonderful years of your friendship.

Do you think I should write a thank you note to Richard Chamberlain, without whose influence we might never have become friends?

I have talked to all of the other tea guests since the party and they all had a wonderful time and were absolutely overwhelmed by all that you did. Everyone loved all of the exotic dishes, including the "curried" egg salad and the chicken/cashew/cherry salad. I don't think any of them guessed about the curry, so the secret is safe unless you blew our cover during teatime conversation! The menu has been propped up on my piano and everyone else who has come in the house this past week has taken a look at it and been blown away by it. Even John Matson, my physical therapist, was very impressed!

… Well, dear friend, that is about it for now. Thank you again for the most wonderful birthday present anyone ever gave me in my whole life!

Love to you and Norm,

Linda

Chapter 14
Angel on My Shoulder

It is hard to conceive that a person stricken with a catastrophic disease could think she had a perpetual "angel on my shoulder," but that is exactly how Linda felt. Amazing as it sounds, Linda *never* felt sorry for herself because of her illness. That is not to say she did not have her moments (always in private) when she hated what ALS was doing to her body and how it had changed her life, but she recognized the importance of a positive attitude throughout her illness. Linda was a fighter, and a woman of great intelligence. She knew that negative feelings would be too destructive to her emotional well-being and her physical health, and she was determined to battle any demons that interfered with her plan to have as "normal" a life as possible under the circumstances.

Linda frequently would mention how her "angel" (who she was convinced was her mother/father) was watching out for her in countless situations that initially seemed to look quite glum. Whether it was an issue with the insurance company, scheduling problems with the home health care services, a Medicare glitch, or something else, in the end, Linda triumphed. I always attributed Linda's victories to her tenacity and spirit, despite the odds. However, Linda was convinced it was that persistent angel on her shoulder!

One of the lowest periods during Linda's illness came toward the end of 2002. Up to that point, the cadre of health care workers who helped her throughout the day had worked out well. However, Linda was getting weaker and her ALS progressing to the point where she knew it was essential for her to acquire more skilled assistance than she was presently receiving. What she really needed was a live-in RN, but that was financially out of the question. Even a nurse who could be with her during the day was too costly for her budget. What to do? Linda checked the ads everyday, and she even placed a few herself. Unless she could find somebody affordable with actual nursing experience, she feared this might be the end of the line for her. This was a real dilemma for Linda, and with every passing day, she expressed more concern.

Finally, at the beginning of the year (2003), there was *some* glimmer of hope. One of her health care workers, Carol, mentioned that she had a sister-in-law who had been living in CA, but was returning to MA very soon. The sister-in-law, Lisa, had actually been a nurse. Sounded perfect – but there was a catch! Lisa was no longer a nurse because she had become a drug addict and her license was revoked. She was also on probation because of her drug addiction. Lisa was trying to get her life back in order. Carol asked Linda if she was willing to take a chance on having Lisa work for her.

What options did Linda have at that time? She needed someone who had nursing training and whom she could afford. After several months of looking and interviewing, nothing had panned out. Linda was in dire need, so she told Carol she was willing to give Lisa a try.

It was only much later that Linda realized her angel had woven the best magic yet to bring together two souls who desperately needed each other and who changed each other's life for the best.

Chapter 15
Intertwined

Lisa Constantino is an integral part of the story of Linda Burge's struggle with ALS. And Linda Burge is an integral part of the story of Lisa Constantino's struggle to sobriety. This was an amazing symbiotic relationship in which each woman pulled the other to new heights, and each felt the power of helping the other in her struggle. In so doing, they both gathered strength to forge ahead in their personal battles.

No one, other than Lisa and Linda, will ever completely fathom their complicated relationship. They laughed together, cried together, confided in one another, got upset with each other, loved each other, and completely depended on each other.

The more Lisa worked for Linda, the more she realized how much she was needed by Linda, and she did not want to disappoint her. For Lisa, that meant staying sober so she could always be there if Linda needed her.

Linda caught onto this situation very early on. After Lisa had been with her a few months, Linda told me that she was now absolutely convinced that the reason she had ALS was to help Lisa get her life back together again. Understanding the reason for her ALS gave Linda great peace of mind. This epiphany also seemed to re-energize her with a new purpose. She now had a mission beyond her ALS – and that was to help Lisa as much as possible so she could take back her life and her career as a nurse.

Linda encouraged Lisa to start thinking about getting reinstated into nursing so she could move on with her life after her probation period. Linda tried to help Lisa in this direction in any way she could, often monetarily. Linda was particularly generous with

Lisa's pay. Even if Lisa came over to do something for 15 minutes, Linda would pay her for the hour. If Lisa stayed to eat a meal with Linda, she would be paid. Occasionally Lisa balked at Linda's overly generous manner, but Linda insisted.

It is remarkable how quickly Linda's quality of life changed after Lisa had been with her for awhile. Lisa is very extroverted and likes to laugh and joke around. This positive aura was not lost on Linda. Linda was a very upbeat person herself, and in concert with Lisa's cheerful personality, it did wonders for Linda's physical well-being.

When Lisa was a nurse, she worked long term with a quadriplegic. Clearly, she had far more experience and knowledge about the needs of a patient like Linda than any of her previous health care workers. Even little things like a scalp massage or a body rub made a big impact on Linda. Nobody had *ever* done these things for her before, and they felt really good! A head scrub or leg and foot massages were not only nourishing Linda's body, but these little incidentals nourished her soul as well. For the first time, Linda felt she had a health care worker who understood her body and knew what to do with her.

Lisa is a take-charge person. She steps up to the plate. After Lisa had been onboard for nearly a year, Linda acquired a new insurance that allowed her to hire her own PCAs (personal care assistants), rather than depend on the less skilled care from the home health care agency. Lisa helped interview all the new hires. She trained all the workers, especially in the use of any new equipment. Though Linda organized the initial scheduling, Lisa later assumed that responsibility.

Linda never let her guard down with other people regarding her ALS. She rarely talked about it with others, and when she did, she monitored what she said. If I hadn't worked so closely with her on this book to chronicle her illness, I, too, would be oblivious to many of the difficulties Linda faced on a daily basis. She put up a good front, and did not feel it was necessary to burden her friends with the details of her illness. On occasion with Lisa however, she was not so guarded. When she was really upset about the loss of another body function, she'd lament that loss and sob, with Lisa joining her in tears. Linda needed that catharsis, and thankfully, she was able to share it with Lisa. Never would she have allowed it with anyone else.

Likewise, Linda was a wonderful sounding board for Lisa. Lisa felt she could talk to Linda about her problems and Linda was a great listener. Linda, as always, was grounded in common sense values, and would share her astute advice when appropriate. Linda encouraged Lisa to bring her two teenaged daughters over to meet Linda when they came to MA for a visit in the summer. Linda, of course, hit it off with both girls, Chelse and Sarah, as well as Lisa's mom, Noel. Linda's solid connection to Lisa's family made their bond even closer.

Another reason for the improvement of Linda's quality of life under Lisa's care was the discovery of the wheelchair van loaner program from Compassionate Care ALS. (Compassionate Care ALS, based in Falmouth, MA, is a support organization for ALS patients and their caregivers.) For several years, Compassionate Care had helped Linda obtain various equipment. One day, Ron Hoffman, Compassionate Care's Director, mentioned they could borrow the wheelchair van for days at a time. All Lisa had to do was drive to Falmouth, leave her car there in exchange for the van, and drive back to Rockland. The only charge would be for the gas.

Prior to this, Linda was basically housebound. With the van from Compassionate Care, a whole new world opened up for Linda. Along with Lisa, she would now have the chance to explore new horizons beyond medical facilities! Even something simple, like a shopping trip to Wal-Mart, was a special treat for Linda. The van gave the duo the opportunity to embark on many new adventures.

~~~~~~~~~~~~~~~~~~~~~~~~~~~~

In the year that Linda and I were working together on this book, she had given me just about all the information we needed to chronicle her illness. She had addressed every topic I requested –

except for one. Whenever I asked her to talk about her history with Lisa, she put it off with one excuse after another. She intended to do a chapter about Lisa, but was never quite "ready." I finally caught on and realized why she kept avoiding the discussion. It was just too emotionally wrenching for her. Once I understood that, I stopped asking and figured Linda would let me know when she was ready to share that part of her story. Unfortunately that time never came. That meant Lisa would have to fill in the missing pieces.

Through the Years

Baby Linda with big sister Judy

Playing with the ducks in NH

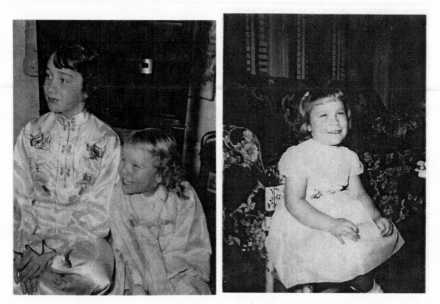

Asian dress up with Judy   Strike a pose!

Bridesmaid at Judy's wedding   Linda's wedding day – with Jim
                                   and her parents

Graduation at Stonehill – with
Jim

Pat and Bonnie with Linda
at the
Cliff Walk

Some of "Linda's Lucky Charms" at their first Cliff
Walk (charity event for ALS) in 2003.

Linda's family at Cliff Walk
(From left – Chris, Susan,
Bernie, Linda, John, & Judy)

With Norm and
Leslie

With Lisa and Elaine

One of Linda's
Birthday Tea
Parties (Linda,
Lisa, Noel,
Maureen,
Catherine,
Santina)

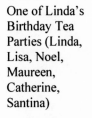

A Night to
Remember:
Linda with Gregg
(far left) at Curt
Schilling's ALS
Reception in
October, 2005.
Curt is in back
row, 3rd from left.

Chapter 16
Here's Lisa!

Since Linda could not bring herself to discuss her relationship with Lisa, the job fell to Lisa herself. In Lisa's interview, she relates a part of her troubled background, goes into her first meeting with Linda, and carries on from there.

Lisa:

Before I came to Massachusetts I was living in California. I had gone through a two year rehab program that was called Delancey Street Foundation. I went in there on May 5, 2000, and I graduated on May 5, 2002. Once you were sentenced there or made the commitment to go there, you had to stay at least two years to be considered a graduate. When you enter Delancey Street, you start your recovery. They consider themselves a "re-educational facility." They reintroduce people to society and society's ethics – especially work ethics. You get up every day and go to work. I decided to stay in San Francisco after I graduated. I had a part-time job; I had an apartment. However, I was floundering. I was all by myself, and I didn't know anybody there. I knew the few people from Delancey Street. I relapsed back into drugs, of course.

I knew I was doing terribly, so I decided I was going to move home to MA. I called up my mom one day and I said, "I need to come home." She was all for it of course, and thought that was great. Naturally, before I left for home I wanted to see my kids (two girls, Sarah and Chelse, ages 14 and 11 at that time) in Fresno. That's just the mother in me. I'd seen them over the summer, but I wanted to visit with them before moving back East. I went to Fresno and I got myself in worse trouble! I was hanging out in the wrong places. I was actually in a house that was raided! Truly, I wasn't doing anything at the time. In fact, at the time of the raid, I was fixing a phone line for a blind man. Not to say I wasn't messing up in any way, but at *that* moment I wasn't doing anything. I ended up going to jail overnight, which consequently delayed my trip home. I should have come home in December, but didn't arrive until January. Before I could leave CA, I had to go to court and get all my legal issues settled. It took a month for the court to say, "Okay you can go home."

I was already on probation in Fresno and Madera and I had gotten permission to come home. That was a long process in itself. Now I had to go and get permission again. They said, "Okay, you can go to MA. You will have to come back to court in a year. If nothing occurs between now and then, we will drop the new charges stemming from being in the wrong place at the wrong time."

I ended up coming back to MA on the 21st or 22nd of January, 2003. I remember my mother was upset because I missed my birthday. I came home and I worked doing house cleaning, little odds and ends for people, or helping out when my mom needed something done. I was mostly working for my mom and not doing much at all.

My sister-in-law Carol, who works for a home health care agency, was working for Linda at the time doing home health care. At that time Linda was not allotted enough hours, so Linda had some other people working for her who were not part of the health care agency. She had someone getting her up in the morning and several people helping her get into bed at night. Linda knew she needed more help, and I guess she mentioned it to Carol. One day Carol called me up and said, "One of my patients is looking for someone to help her a couple of nights a week putting her to bed. She is going to need more help in the future, but right now she just needs a little extra assistance."

Carol had told Linda that I had a drug problem, and that I was trying to change my life. That was at the beginning of February, 2003, so I hadn't even been home for three weeks. Carol said, "Do you want to come with me one night and I will show you what we do? I'll go through the whole routine." I agreed, we set up a time, and she was going to introduce me to Linda.

I met Carol at Linda's. It's funny, because when I went to the house, I remember being very nervous because it had been a long time since I'd worked in the health care system as a nurse. I didn't know what to expect. I never knew anybody with ALS. All I knew of ALS was what they taught us in school – very little. The mother of one of my girlfriends had passed away from Lou Gehrig's disease. I always knew what Lou Gehrig's was - in a way - but I never related ALS with Lou Gehrig's. I just knew it was a horrific disease, and it was difficult for my friend to watch her mother go through it. Her mom passed away very quickly. That's all I knew of Lou Gehrig's disease. I figured – okay – ALS - whatever. How hard could this be?

Linda would have told you that when I got there the very first time, I had my hand on the doorknob, and I was like a deer caught in the headlights! I had this look of terror on my face! It's true, I *was* very frightened, and I thought, "Oh no! What am I getting myself into?" Little did I know! I finally let go of the doorknob (!), went in, and Carol began to go over the routine. At that time Linda was operating her wheelchair with her hand, so she drove it to the bathroom door. She could still stand up and transfer to the commode chair. We'd get her ready for bed there, and then she would transfer back to the wheelchair. Linda's bathroom wasn't very big, so you can imagine the wheelchair in the bathroom, the walker, the commode chair, and an assistant! You couldn't be big! Carol showed me how to brush Linda's teeth and went through the rest of the routine. I don't remember her showing me how to put Linda in bed. I believe we set up for the first night right after that. I don't remember if I was coming that night to put her to bed. I guess I put her to bed so many times it's just like a blur. We arranged it so that I was going to work two nights a week – I think it was Mondays and Wednesdays. The other girl was not working out too well. Linda had to call her up and remind her to come all the time. I think Nancy was doing two nights then, too. I don't know who was doing the rest.

The very first night I was getting her ready for bed, there was a lot of tension. I didn't know Linda, she didn't know me, and I was doing – as Linda called it – "intimate work:" cleaning her, helping her wipe herself, etc. I was brushing Linda's teeth, and me being me, I am always cracking jokes. I couldn't even tell you what I said, but it made Linda start choking on the toothpaste. So when she finally gathered herself together, she looked me dead straight in the eye, and she said, "People with ALS choke on their own. They don't need any help!"

I thought, "Okay – I will try to keep the humor to a point!" That pretty much broke the ice. That was the first time I can remember thinking, "Oh my God – I'm going to choke the poor girl to death!"

At the beginning, that was how I started out with Linda – doing the bedtime routine. I went over in the evening, helped her put her pajamas on, cleaned her up – her face, her teeth, helped her on the toilet, and got her into her bed. The extent of the help was dependent on what she was able to do. That's kind of all a blur now, because I don't remember exactly what she could or couldn't do when I first started. I do know when I put her into bed, I would set her up. She would have her intercom system and the automatic door lock to unlock the front door – those were placed within reach. I would hand her the remote for the TV. I don't remember if she could use the phone at that time. She was still feeding herself then, so she had some use of her right hand.

The bedtime routine soon expanded into coming over and helping to get her dinner ready sometimes. Then I was going over in the afternoon to do a bathroom run. I wasn't there for more than ten minutes, but she was paying me for an hour. Somehow the physical therapy came up and I said, "You know, you're paying me for an hour. I could be doing some of your physical therapy. I could be doing more." She agreed that was a good idea. When her physical therapist John came over, he'd show me the exercises. John was coming three days a week, and Linda wanted to do about three days more. So now when I would go over in the afternoon for a bathroom trip, we would do some PT. She was still doing a lot of moving of her legs and arms at that point. She could still lift her arms over her head.

Little by little, I was working with Linda more and more. I had started off with two nights, then went to helping with dinner, then doing a bathroom run along with her exercises. I cannot remember how the timeline worked for that, though.

The timeline must have moved fairly quickly because Linda had felt she was in dire straights before Lisa came. She was very much aware that she needed a lot more home care, and a lot more skilled care. So as long as Lisa could handle whatever Linda threw at her, they just kept adding to the mix.

It's almost funny looking back now as we progressed to each step. It was like a little test came each time. A little bit more got thrown in my hands, and I thought, "I can handle this." That stands out in my mind so vividly.

One of my very early experiences is quite memorable. When Linda was in the bathroom and she was finished, I got her cleaned up. Linda stood up so I could clean her, then she sat down. At that point, she was ready to transfer to the wheelchair, but she could only transfer in one direction, which was clockwise. Even though the walker and the wheelchair were next to each other, she'd still have to turn all the way around to sit back down because she could not turn counter clockwise to the two chairs at the right angle. It was a long trek. She was doing that and one leg and foot stayed still – the right leg didn't move as well as the left leg. She kept stepping around and around and around.

She got halfway there, maybe three quarters of the way, and she said, "I can't move. I can't do anything." I am very quick on my feet, and I said, "All right. This is what we are going to do. I am going to move the walker, grab you, and put you in the chair." Linda didn't even have time to answer me, but I moved everything out of the way, grabbed Linda by her pants, and literally threw her into the chair. Looking back now I couldn't even tell you what I did with that walker. I do remember my knee getting clipped on that one! Linda was not a little person. Granted, she wasn't in the chair all the way. She was slouched over, and the look on her face was like, "Now what are you going to do?" I told her I was going to lift her up little by little and keep adjusting her in the chair, so I kept pivoting her like that until she was full in the chair. The sigh of relief after that – for both of us – was palpable! Thank God I didn't put her on the floor! Right then and there, Linda knew what she was dealing with, and she said. "You're good. You're quick, and you're what I need."

Gradually things like that happened. That was the first time, and I thought to myself, "What did she do when I wasn't there?" Of course we all know that she fell, and the falls were happening more frequently. Before, she would fall when she was alone, but now she was falling even when she had an assistant present. Obviously, some of that assistance was not what it should have been. I react very quickly to things, so when she started to fall with me, I caught her right away. You need to have quick reflexes working with someone like Linda.

My first summer, we were counter-balancing the schedule with the home health care agency. I forget how many mornings a week they were coming, maybe four mornings a week they would come and get her ready. Now as I think of it, they did not come very early – about 9:00 or so. By the time they came to shower her and clean her up, etc., I already had her up and in the chair. The girl that had been coming early in the morning to get her up for the bathroom, couldn't do it any more, so I took over more of those responsibilities. There were still a couple of people who did come early to get her out of bed at around 7:30. I, as well as some of the other aides, counter balanced whatever the health care agency didn't do – getting dinner ready, etc. At that point, she could still feed herself. As long as the food was out or heated up and prepared, she could eat it herself without assistance. She also had a housekeeper who did some cleaning for her. There were a lot of people helping out at that time, and I was just one of them, working part time.

It was during this time that the home health care agency was starting to have trouble moving her and keeping her on her feet. In retrospect, I can see that the home health care agency had legal concerns about the care they offered Linda – especially since she was prone to falling. Who knows what is going to transpire? They didn't want to worry about someone getting hurt on their watch, and Linda was becoming too difficult for them to handle. At one point they told her "Lisa needs to be there every time one of our girls is there, because we can't move you on your own." So again, as things were getting more and more difficult for Linda, I was seeing her more often.

I remember the day Linda said to me, "I can't lift my arms up anymore." Then she broke down and cried. She realized, "Oh my gosh - another chip." We got through the moment, then laughed about it. Linda and I had many laughs and many tears. The first time she broke down and cried, I cried right along with her, and I was still fairly new with her – less than six months. I don't remember what it was at the time – most likely the loss of another function. I remember that in trying to help her out of the moment, I attempted to inject some humor into the situation. Then she began to apologize, and said she was sorry she let her guard down, etc. I let her know right away that it was okay if she needed to cry, but she had to realize that I was going to cry right along with her. I think that became a relief to her – knowing she could have those unguarded moments with me and allow her emotions to spill out.

It was definitely a relief to Linda because <u>never</u> would she do that in front of anybody else.

My mom was my sounding board for a lot of my experiences with Linda when I was frazzled. I can remember going home and telling my mom, "That was a trip. Linda just let loose and started crying. I felt good that I was there for her." It was almost like a badge of honor that I could be there and be the shoulder to cry on and help her get through it by ultimately making some joke that would get us both laughing.

Another example of how our relationship evolved is when Linda could no longer order out for food as she had in the past. There would be no way for her to take out the food once it arrived and serve it to herself. She would tell me she was going to buy Chinese food, and ask if I would like to come over and watch a movie - or whatever. This approach not only helped Linda retain her sense of dignity despite her increasing disabilities, but it also helped cement our relationship. The bond grew so quickly.

I can't ever imagine anyone being quite like Linda. She was such a likable person – and so giving. We would argue about money. I would argue that she would pay me an hour's wage for ten minutes work. I would tell her that I had to do something for the money – clean, anything, whatever. That's how she was – she was very generous like that. She would never invite me over to have Chinese food and allow me to pay. So we would argue about that!

~~~~~~~~~~~~~~~~~~~~~~~

When Linda was having trouble transferring from the commode to the wheelchair, she started doing research to see if there was better equipment out there to suit her needs. Through her research she discovered the sliding chair, which I think she got shortly after I arrived on the scene. She got it from Compassionate Care, Ron Hoffman's group. Ron came up to oversee the installation. At the time, he said something about having a van that was available to borrow for a day or days at a time. When we heard about this, I remember standing in Linda's kitchen and saying, "We could go somewhere!" and she, like a little kid, asked, "Wow – we could?" I told her we could get the van and make plans to have an outing. I am sure in the back of her head, she was thinking, "Hmm. Am I going to be okay with this woman taking me around in a van?" Don't forget we hadn't known each other very long at that point. Of course I was thinking, "What am I getting myself into?"

Keep in mind that Linda rarely got out of her condo, except to go to the occasional medical appointment. She hated being so isolated, as it was not Linda's nature to be a homebody. She always loved getting out and going places. Though she accepted

83

her homebody status and never complained about it, occasionally
she would wistfully remark about a particular place that she
wished she could visit.

When I first came there was still snow on the ground, and I took her out for a walk in the wheelchair on Hingham St. She hadn't done that before. She would go out around the condo complex, but that was it. When we went out into the neighboring area beyond the condo for the first time, she was totally energized. "Wow! That was great!"

Linda actually looked forward to her medical appointments because it meant an opportunity to leave the confines of her condo. For her it was literally getting out into the world.

The first time we got the van, we went to Gail's brother's wake in Plymouth. I had to drive to Falmouth to get the van. I was quite adventurous, and this whole idea of being able to transport Linda was very exciting. On the way to the wake in Plymouth, we drove along the coast, and then she had me pull into Burt's restaurant. Keep in mind that Linda was the real driver of the van – I was just maneuvering the vehicle! She would always direct me. After pulling into Burt's, the next thing I knew, Linda was sitting at the beach, absolutely glowing, and basking in the glory of being at the ocean again. You know, she never lost that same glow every time we went on a trip in the van. Even on a trip to Wal-Mart, that glow just covered her being. It was the joy of being out – of celebrating life beyond the walls of her little abode.

I fed off the happiness that permeated Linda's being on these trips. When you see positive results from something, you want to do it more. I couldn't get enough of it for Linda.

Despite the success of the van on that first trip, it was quite awhile before we got it again and made a regular habit of borrowing it. However, other arrangements were made for several other outings after that – once to a baby shower, and once to a piano recital. Sometimes Linda would go places using Bill's Taxi, but that was $250 a pop – very expensive.

That first summer we had the van for a week and we had a yard sale at my house. Linda had her own table and she sold her own things. That experience made her feel like she was doing something normal, despite her ALS.

It was always so much fun to go out in the van. Taking Linda out was like taking a little kid because she loved it so much. So many times we would do something and she would comment, "I never thought I'd be doing this again." She loved to go places, she loved to go out to eat, she loved to go meet her friends. I did things too that I never thought I would do! Whoever thought I would go to a garden party wearing a straw hat and a dress? I did a lot of things that I had never done before on those outings with Linda – going to the mansions in Newport, driving around Hull gut. We made many trips to the water. I had never been up to Gloucester and Rockport. We went to Little Compton, RI, one of Linda's favorite places.

When we had the van, we started going out to restaurants right off the bat, too. The first time we had the vehicle we went out to eat because Linda hadn't been to a restaurant in so long. I remember Linda talking about an experience she had in a restaurant long before she had ALS. She was with some people eating dinner in a restaurant and had seen a gentleman in a wheelchair a few tables away who was being fed by another member of his party. What made an indelible impression upon her was that everyone in the gentleman's group seemed very natural about it. I can remember when we went out in a group with Linda in her wheelchair, and I asked her, "Are you okay with me feeding you?" That's when she told me the story, and a result, it just never bothered her. Now believe me, we got stares because not everyone is used to that. However, we would just laugh it off and say to each other, "Hey, check out that guy!" We actually had people come up to us and say, "You guys are having so much fun. I would rather be sitting at your table!" So eating out became a normal thing for us and never bothered either one of us. I think my comfort level assisted her comfort level and vice versa. That would always make the transition of things that much easier.

When we did start taking the van regularly, it was a major event, because we would always think, "Okay – what can we jam into this week we have the van?" Also, there were many times I would offer to take Linda out, and then she would pay me. Linda was still paying me from her own funds at this time. I would feel bad because it was my suggestion to go some place. It was almost like, "Let's go do this and you can pay me." That was certainly not my intention, but I would go through that whole guilt thing.

I was working a job I loved, and I was making money. Yet I felt I needed to do more real work. I felt guilty when I was driving Linda around and I was having fun. However, Linda cherished that, and she was willing to pay for her freedom.

Our relationship catapulted from me doing a simple bedtime routine to doing physical therapy and everything else. By the end of my first year with Linda, it seemed like everybody was physically dropping Linda. I will say it on record right now – Linda never fell on me. Never. She may have started to, but she never hit the ground with me. Granted, some of those semi-falls weren't graceful: me getting her to that bed or to that chair. That was a tremendous thing for me – never to let that happen. I thank God it never did. I think it would have devastated me.

That's when the home health care agency was fading out. If a worker from the agency was there, I was there because they wouldn't make the transfers alone. It was really ridiculous because I could do it on my own, so why did we need them? All of Linda's own people who did not work for the home health care agency could work the equipment, yet the agency people couldn't. Linda really lost a lot of faith in the agency as a result of that. They never sent anybody over who was capable enough or could handle all the equipment. They couldn't even handle the shower chair which was the easiest of all the equipment.

In late fall of the first year I was here, Linda started applying for Mass Health. I think one of the social workers from the home health care agency had come in and got her going on it. You have to qualify for the PCA (Personal Care Assistant) program. I wasn't in on all that. I assisted a little, but she orchestrated it all on her own with Mass Health. It was a really good thing because she was going to go broke paying me!

I never totally knew Linda's finances, though I know more about them now because I helped Judy when she took over after Linda was gone. I know what Judy said Linda used to have, and what she ended up with. I can tell you where a lot of that money went. There were some weeks when I made $800. It was a lot of money for me. Certainly it was a lot of money for me to have and not use for dope! As a nurse I made that and used every bit on drugs. I had a very expensive habit. But now, finally, I was getting back on my feet. I was able to pay off debts and put money aside. I also had fines when I came out here, but I was resolving those as well. I was still on probation up until 2004.

Leslie: Were you ever tempted to go back to drugs?
Lisa: Not here.
Leslie: What do you attribute that to?
Lisa: Support.

When I first came back as part of my probation I had to do an out patient program. I did it in Brockton at Gosnold-Thorne, an outpatient recovery facility. It was a three month program. I had to agree to that before my probation officers would let me leave CA. I saw a therapist there in Brockton, and I asked her why I was doing better here. She said my standards were higher here, and I had more people to let down, face to face. It was one thing to let my mother down three thousand miles away, but it was another thing to let her down while I was with her. Also, I had the love of friends and family. In addition to all my friends, I had all Linda's friends, too. A lot of people looked up to me, including Linda. Linda was right up there with my mom as one whom I could not let down. I had money coming in, but I had gas to buy as well as other things. I was paying off my fines and starting to feel good. I felt that I had a purpose. When Linda came into my life, I truly believe she became my purpose in life. We all want to feel needed and wanted, and I felt like that was what I needed to be doing. Linda and I laughed many times about who really got us together. Somebody orchestrated that. It wasn't a chance happening. She needed help. I needed help. Whether it was my stepfather who had passed away or Linda's mother, I don't know. Linda and I used to say, "They are up there collaborating to get us together!" Even to her dying day we both talked about it. It was meant to be. I have joked and told her, "Well if I hadn't screwed up, you wouldn't have met me!" Linda said it was a good thing I didn't meet her before she had ALS because we both probably could have done some major damage!

So no, the drug thing wasn't really tempting, but then I didn't know anybody around here who was using anything. Some of my friends drink, but that was never my problem, and not a temptation. The longer I am away from anything, the stronger I am. I attribute my strength to somebody upstairs now.

Linda very quickly became a part of our family. My mom took a shining to her right away. My mother had heard about Linda through my sister-in-law. Mom knew Carol took care of an ALS patient in Rockland and that was it. It was through my sister-in-law that Linda knew who Sarah and Chelse were because they used to come here for the summer. Carol would tell her that her nieces were coming here from CA. Linda already knew some of my family through Carol. It's kind of funny how she then became part of the family herself. Linda looked at my mother like *her* mother. My mother did many motherly things for her. Linda was just one of those people you want to take in and make them a part of your life. If we had the van, I would bring her over to the house and we'd cook hot dogs on the grill, or whatever. When my girls came home that first summer, Linda and I went and did things with them. So now the girls were part of *her* family. Linda loves kids, so when my girls came over Linda's, it was a great thing. I can remember her just glowing seeing me with my girls, and knowing that she was part of that connection. Now I was in a place where I could have my kids in my life, and that meant a lot to Linda, too.

Linda knew how much play she had on my life, and she knew what she was taking on. She liked to compare it to this lifeboat story. A person is on top of his roof in a flood and he is praying for help. First somebody in a canoe comes along and offers help. The guy declines and says he'll wait. Then somebody in a rowboat comes along, and the guy on the roof declines his help. Now the water is practically up to the roof, and a person in a motorboat comes to help. The guy on the roof once again declines, saying he'll wait. Finally the water is up to the roof and the guy drowns. He complains to God that he didn't send him any help. God said that he sent the canoe, the rowboat, and the motorboat. The guy said, "Well I was waiting for the cruise ship with the lifeboat."

Linda used to say *I* was her lifeboat. I did feel all that taking care of her. It was something I could do and do well. I had taken care of a quadriplegic before and changed his life. He was a guy who *never* went out. He had been a quad for ten years, and progressed to not going out any more and staying in bed. I came on as his RN after just graduating. I said, "Come on, get out of bed. Let's do something." In the year I took care of him, I had him up in the truck driving around going places. So it wasn't something I was unfamiliar with, without even realizing it. Linda knew that I had experience taking care of a quad. He had a trache. He had bedsore wounds that I cleaned. I did everything as a nurse. Gradually Linda would get this information, so she knew I had the skills that she needed. Linda used to tell a lot of the people we would interview that I had a lot of experience with quads. Many of those skills came back for me when I needed them for Linda. When the care got more intense, I could tell myself, "Oh yes, I still know how to do that." As for the equipment, I am very mechanically inclined, so that helped. Linda called me "smarter than the average bear!" That was a good thing because she had a lot of mechanical equipment at the end.

By the end of the first year, I was working seven days a week for Linda. My kids were not living with me then. I had something to do. It was great. I would work two hours here, two hours here, two hours here. It's not like my whole day was taken up, and I couldn't do other things. I was doing three or four different jobs. That was until I started working about 30 hours a week for Linda.

When she got Mass Health at the end of the year, we were looking for some kind of equipment to lift her because she was falling too frequently. We knew she needed to get appropriate equipment that would lift her in and out of the chair, in and out of bed, etc. On her own, through her research, Linda was able to find the pivot lift. If she hadn't made an aggressive search, she never would have found it because the information just isn't out there.

Once she got the Mass Health, the home health care agency was out, and she was on her own to hire people. Mass Health gave her per week: 59 ¼ hours during the day and 14 hours for nights. We actually started the interviewing process for PCAs before Mass Health had come through. I was going to court in CA in January, so we were trying to get everything in place before I left. Linda and I did the interviewing and the training together. There was a good response to the ads. Right after Christmas, we trained four people. We trained Nancy, the nighttime girl, for other shifts. We trained Tina, Darlene, and Shauna. All the training was very painstaking and tiring for both of us, but we felt we had a good crew. By the time I went to CA for the five days in January, the new workers were already in place and pretty much trained. The pivot lift came while I was gone, but I think only Shauna was using the lift. Unfortunately, Linda fell a couple of times while I was gone.

Linda was a very good manager. She did most of the scheduling and fit all the workers in to best accommodate her routine. I wrote it all up, but it was in her head. The same with all the time cards. Gradually, things became more and more my responsibility. Linda referred to me as the "Chief Attendant," so I oversaw all the other workers, the scheduling, and the time cards. Linda also made it very clear to all the workers that I was the leader, and the one they had to answer to other than Linda herself.

Even when I was in CA, I was "on call." There were many times when I would get a call because Linda was only half way in the chair and the worker couldn't get her all the way in the chair. When I returned home, I was definitely on call for everything. If anybody didn't show up, I would have to deal with it. Linda was now my primary job. To me it didn't even feel like a job because it was such a friendship. I could go there in a bad mood and come

90

away in a great mood. She would always make things seem wonderful. If she was living with ALS, nothing in my life could be that bad.

She saw me through all the little triumphs in my life, like when I got off my probation period in CA. My mother gave me the title to the truck I was driving, which had been my stepfather's. Linda saw all those little milestones in my life, and I cherish those little things that she gave back to me. I know I worked hard, but Linda opened that door for me, when I had no doors open. At the time, I didn't know what I was coming home to. I had no job. First I planned to work with my brother and go into the pipe fitting business. I was not young, but he could have gotten me in. He said the reason he did not get me in was because there are a lot of drugs in the union, and he was afraid for me. That's what he told me after I got home. That's when he said, "Nah, you don't want to go into the union. Stick with the nursing." Thank God Linda came along, because I was cleaning houses, and that's hard work! Going to work for Linda never felt like it was hard work. It was more light-hearted, and then there was the friendship. I felt like I was being paid to be a companion sometimes.

After I had been there for about a year, Linda was no longer able to feed herself. I don't think she could even raise her right arm. I began picking up a lot of the mealtime shifts. The schedule dictated that someone be there to get her up in the morning, get her bathed, dressed, and cleaned up. Someone had to be there for lunch, then later in the afternoon for a bathroom break. Then there was dinner, and bedtime. It ended up working into four shifts throughout the day. The morning person would stay through breakfast and sometimes lunch. Then the afternoon bathroom break, then dinner, then bed. A lot of those shifts were quick – less than on hour. The morning shift was the longest. It normally took a minimum of two hours. Anytime we hired a new person, it would take them three hours to do that shift. We also had to make sure we could fit everyone into the time allotted by Mass Health. The time always got used up.

Linda was always one step ahead of her disease, and that taught me a lot. You really need to look beyond today. She was always ready. She was ready with the pivot lift, she was ready with the shower chair. She did her research before she *had* to. She never succumbed to the inevitable and prided herself on the fact that she got up, bathed, and dressed every day. Not one day went by that she stayed in bed. Even when she didn't feel well, she made herself get up and dressed for the day. That was a very big thing. Once she was up and in the wheelchair, that was it. She was up for the rest of the day. On several occasions, I was able to convince her it was okay to lie in bed in the middle of the day and watch a little TV. So she did that a couple of times, and it always felt like a luxury to her. I would prop her up with pillows so she could lie on her side, which she loved, but rarely got to do because she couldn't do it herself.

It was the same with hugging somebody. She couldn't do that anymore. From the beginning she and I were huggy-touchy. I would get her up in the morning and take her arms and put them behind my back and hold them, then hug her so her arms were there too. She would squeeze. You could feel it in her shoulders. Things like that would set her off occasionally. She told me that she missed the fact that she couldn't hug people anymore. That's probably why I got into the routine of helping her to hug me. Not everybody was comfortable enough hugging Linda on their own, so sometimes I would actually put her arms around them. I'd say, "Linda wanted to hug you." People were sometimes afraid to get close to her. I'm sure it bothered Linda. The more her disease progressed, the less likely people were to reach into her wheelchair to make physical contact with her. I used to feel for her because her family was not a huggy-touchy family, and they would leave without giving her a hug. To me, when you leave after visiting, you hug somebody goodbye. Bernie (her niece's husband) would give her a hug, or her brother-in-law John might, but her sister didn't. I discussed this with Linda, and though she didn't admit it, I know it must have bothered her.

When I first met Linda her sister Judy would come down, but she was always afraid to feed her. As time went on, she was able to do that to a certain extent, but she was still afraid. Judy's biggest fear was that Linda would choke while she was feeding her, but she would never say that to Linda. When I was there, Judy had a greater comfort level. Linda choked on me – more than once. I fell apart... afterwards. I was very good in the moment, but I broke down afterwards. It's very scary. So I could understand her sister being afraid. I know it was sometimes hard for Linda to deal with her family's reaction to her disease. Linda realized her family loved her, but they could not help the way they dealt with this family trauma. I kept telling Linda that it was not personal. No matter who had the issue in the family, the reaction would have been the same. I know Linda came to accept that. They did come around more and more. They would always ask for me to be there, as my presence helped them feel more comfortable around Linda, just in case anything happened. That was fine with me.

Chapter 17
Equipment

Linda:

It is critical for disabled people to know that there is appropriate, adaptive equipment out there, but no one is going to come knocking on your door to tell you about it. You must be proactive. I have made it a habit of scanning over *every* newsletter and publication that comes my way just to see if something catches my eye that might be helpful. Once I was reading either the Cliff Walk or the ALS newsletter, and it mentioned that if you needed any equipment, they have a lending program. It mentioned a *sliding shower chair*. I asked several people about it, but no one knew what this equipment was. I called the organization and they described it, but they did not have one available at that time. They put me in contact with the company that made the sliding shower chair. They sent me a brochure and followed up with an in-home demo. I knew this would be a very useful piece of equipment for me, and I ultimately purchased it. It is non-motorized, works by body strength, and is very easy to operate. The sliding shower chair has become a major component in my home care. Unfortunately, insurance does not consider bathroom equipment important enough to be a covered expense. Blue Cross and Medicare consider commodes and shower equipment to be "luxury" items. It cost about $2700. To acquire the equipment I had to front the total price, but I was reimbursed for most of it. I called the Cliff Walk organization and asked them if they could help at all. They gave me $1300 toward the cost. Ron Hoffman of Compassionate Care/Gordon T. Heald Fund donated another $600, and Interfaith Charity in Quincy donated $500. When all was said and done, my out of pocket expense was $300.

The sliding shower chair is a rolling commode seat that attaches to a frame that slides you on that same seat right into the shower. My caregiver moves me from my bed or wheelchair onto a rolling chair that has a toilet seat. I get rolled into the bathroom and the chair slides right over the regular toilet. It eliminates the need to transfer to the toilet seat. There is a metal frame the seat hooks onto so it can be pushed into the shower. It is very simple and terrific because I can be showered and toileted easily with no extra transfers. There is one move from wheelchair to the sliding shower chair. This equipment has increased my safety and made my life a whole lot easier, yet no one seemed to know anything about it. I am so glad that I just happened upon the article that mentioned this chair and I followed up on it. This is a perfect example of why one has to be proactive and seek information about any equipment or accommodation that could be of value.

Another thing I came across was the lift equipment that is used now to get me in and out of bed, the wheelchair, and the commode/shower chair. My physical therapist had heard about this lift, but he had never seen it. We sent for a video demo, watched it and tried to figure out how it would apply to my disability. We arranged for an in-home demo, and eventually ordered it. It is called an *easy pivot lift machine*. It is non-motorized and operated by body strength. It is very, very safe, and quite easy to train a caregiver to use it properly.

Amazingly, this safe and easy to use lift is not commonly used. I cannot understand why.

What is commonly used is a piece of equipment called a Hoyer lift. Though the Hoyer is used almost everywhere, it has many drawbacks. It is unsafe unless you have two caregivers operating it, yet it is often used by only one caregiver. It can tip. I think it's quite scary. The pivot lift is used easily by one assistant regardless of size. One of my caregivers weighs about 90 pounds. She got me up with no trouble and no injury to herself or to me.

The pivot lift was invented by a quadriplegic. He knew what he needed. I ended up ordering it directly from the manufacturer in Colorado. No one around here deals with it. John, my physical therapist, found out about it because someone dropped a brochure off at his office. The easy pivot lift was only $1700. More than half the cost was covered by Medicare and Blue Cross.

So, you really need to keep your eyes open. When I see *anything* about equipment, if there is even a remote possibility that it could help me, I always try to investigate.

Reading has always been one of the great pleasures of my life. When I could no longer handle a book, I was able to acquire a book page turner. The device sits atop a small easel. The book is inserted into the device which has a rubber roller in the middle. The roller moves from side to side to turn pages, and it is controlled by a joystick. The page turner works much better on hard cover books, not as well on paperbacks. I was able to use this for reading until I could no longer operate the joystick.

I would advise anyone who needs a power wheelchair to try to get all the bells and whistles at the time you order it, even if you don't need them at that time. Once you do need to revamp or adapt, it is complicated, takes a long time, and you must deal with insurance yet again. I regret I did not do this when I first ordered my power chair.

As my disease progressed within the past year, I realized that my ability to operate my chair by using the joystick was coming to an end, so I began my quest of finding a vendor who could retrofit this chair with head controls. It was a challenge. I called many, many vendors. They all knew what I wanted, but none of them were able to provide it. Ultimately, I called Ron Hoffman at Compassionate Care, Gordon T. Heald Fund and I asked Ron if he knew of anyone who could help. Ron asked why I hadn't called him first! He put me in touch with Spaulding Rehabilitation Hospital in Boston, and I went in for an evaluation for what they call a wheelchair clinic. The wheelchair physical therapist met me there with a vendor, and ordered what should take me to the end of the line. There are so many different kinds of controls. Chris Reeve had what was called a sip and puff control. He sucked on a straw and his breath was used to control the chair. I can't do that because I don't have the lip control. The head control works for me. My speed, forward, reverse, and all of the other features are in the headrest. All I do is move my head to tell my chair what I need. Spaulding was able to order a new seating arrangement for my chair that will tilt the back of the seat so it can lay flat or can sit up straighter. They ordered leg rests that will raise and lower at will, which also is very important because when you are immobile with your legs bent at the knee all the time, blood clots are a big issue. Now my retrofitted wheelchair with all of this revamping is wonderful and allows me more mobility.

This revamped wheelchair has a little computer-type screen on an extension from the wheelchair arm. It's probably about 5" X 5". I can use that as a visual guide to confirm what I am trying to do with the wheelchair. If I hit the head control and I get an audible beeping sound, that will tell me whether I have changed directions, or I'm in forward or reverse. I can confirm visually by looking at the read-out on the screen before I move and make a mistake. It also has a read-out for the additional features, the tilt, the backrest, leg rests, and the speed you are in. It's a help and a safety feature to be able to see what the computer says you are doing before you put the chair in motion. The leg rest can extend up and down, both legs simultaneously or separately, and you can combine the adjustments. I can raise both to a certain height and if I find I am not completely comfortable, perhaps I will raise my right leg higher. Then I hit the headrest and watch until the screen advises me my right leg is able to adjust. Next, I hit the headrest to raise or lower that one leg. I decided to retain the joystick function. Even though I can no longer use it, my caregivers are able to walk along beside me and power the chair through the joystick, or fine-tune my location. Recently I had a dental appointment, and Lisa used the joystick to position the chair in the exam room around the dental equipment. It would have been a little tricky with the head controls.

For some reason, there is a fluke in this system and every once in a while when I power off in the lowest speed, the next time I power up, I am in the highest speed. They have been unable to find out what is causing the problem. So whenever I power up I look at the screen to make sure what speed is registering. I can the lower the speed if necessary. Now I have become accustomed to look before I drive!

One evening when I had the newly revamped chair only about a week, and it was operating with no problems, I was in my bedroom in a space about two feet wide between the side of the bed and my patio sliding door. I was watching the TV. I turned the chair on to move and I found myself doing revolutions at high, high speed. The chair had come up in the high speed and I was unable to shut it down because the head motion to shut it off passed the head motion to turn. So I was doing 360s in a very narrow space. I hit the window. Why it didn't break I'll never know. I hit the bed and knocked it way out of line. Ultimately, I ended up moving forward with my head as I was fearful of touching the headrest again and setting off another firestorm. I was sitting with my head forward like that for about two hours until Lisa showed up to put me to bed. She walked in and said, "Oh my God, what happened?" However, now I know what to do if that happens. I immediately lower the speed. Since then, the vendor sent a tech out here and they have cut the power by about half. So, if by some chance, the chair gets out of my control, it's at a lesser speed.

~~~~~~~~~~~~~~~~~~~~~~~~~~~~

For anyone with ALS or any fast moving disease, time is a critical factor. The wheels of everything around you move very slowly while the disease is galloping along. When it comes to equipment or services, you need to put them in place long before you anticipate using or needing them. Another example of this is my new computer, which is a technological marvel. I expect it will become the center of my universe as it eventually will be my voice and assist me in numerous everyday functions. We were first introduced to this type of assistive technology in October of '04 at Spaulding Rehab.

When I called to make the appointment for revamping my wheelchair, I complimented the woman on the phone who took all my info because she communicated with me and had no problem with my compromised speech. She said, "It's my job." She asked me if I would have any interest in meeting with the speech and occupational speech therapist to see if they could put together a package of voice assisted equipment. I figured, sure, why not. I totally thought there would be very little they could offer. Well, I was wrong because my new computer will do everything that any other computer does, plus it will speak for me when ALS takes away my voice.

We first went in to meet with them in October of '04 and here it is May of '05. It took all that time to get the equipment. Fortunately I had the time. Many people with ALS do not have seven months, so I cannot encourage anyone under those circumstances. That is why I am such an advocate of being proactive and looking ahead toward future needs. Get what you might need when you *don't* need it because by the time it is delivered to you, you probably will need it. Almost invariably, the biggest hang-up and time warp is due to insurance. It takes forever for the bureaucracy to approve all the claims.

Ways the new computer will change my life
This computer will do everything a regular PC will do: internet, online banking and shopping, etc. I can play a DVD and control all the functions, which I cannot do anymore on a regular DVD because I cannot use the remote. I can play music on it and select the track I want to listen to. With the use of a head mouse, I can control the functions of the computer. The head mouse is a small metallic sticker, less than the size of a paper punch hole, that you can wear on your glasses, forehead, the brim of a cap, or anything on your head. On the top of the computer's display screen, there is a clip-on gadget that is the size of a small digital camera, and it picks up the infrared reflection from the dot on my forehead, and it moves the cursor around the screen. When the movement on my head moves the cursor and the mouse is on what they call a twell click, and when I find what I want to click on, I just settle the cursor on it for an elapsed period of time and the mouse clicks and selects that item. The speed of that is controlled by me. The better I get, the faster I can do it. This computer has built in programs of directives for my care. In other words, I can easily select such

orders as "I want to eat. I need the bathroom. I'm tired. I'm cold. I'm hot, etc." And those come up with a very simple click. My caregiver can know what I need. With one of the software programs I can also carry on a spoken conversation. I type out what I want to say. Many of the words commonly used in our language are built into the program, so I don't need to type out "today;" I click on the word "today." It saves a lot of time and energy. It will speak what I am writing. When ALS makes my speech completely unintelligible, the computer will speak my thoughts. I will be able to download books, best sellers, etc. It costs $15 annually for all the books I want to read. With the head mouse, turning pages will be easy. I will able to write letters, print them, and US Mail them. I will be able to e-mail. There is a way that this computer will make a telephone call for me and speak my message to the person I am calling. Also it has a feature called X-10 that will turn lights on and off, turn the TV on and off. I believe it will change channels on the TV. I have a lot to learn. I've only been working on it for a few days and when I initially got it, it was set up in a demo mode that shut me out after twenty minutes. It has only been two days since the set up has changed so I do not get shut out, and with very little practice, I have already learned a great deal.

At such time when I can no longer speak, that screen can be mounted on the wheelchair. I have the equipment to do it right now. However, when people transfer me to and from the chair, it's one more thing that would be an impediment, could get broken, etc. So right now, while I am mobile with the wheelchair, I have decided to set this up in a stationary location on my computer desk. For the future, I think all you need is a wireless router to put it on the chair and take it anywhere you go.

For software on the computer, I'm using Word Pad, which is comparable to a Microsoft Word, but it is enhanced with a word prediction function. I am also using something called Word Pro, which is the communication software that will speak what I write. That one also can be customized. For example, I have my sister's name on a key. If you hit that it tells you that she is my health care proxy. The other program I had some fun with that is similar to the

100

Word Pro is called QWERTY. It's also quite useful for communication.

I know another ALS patient, Ed, and his wife, Donna. They communicate with each other through a letter board that Donna made. It is laborious, but it works amazingly well for Ed and Donna because they are in sync. Donna points to the letters and Ed blinks when she selects the letter he wants. For anyone else to try to communicate like that would be a big challenge. Donna made one of these boards for me. I was amazed she would do that. Lisa and I have played with it. When Lisa and I use it, it's frightening, as she seems to read my mind! So we have limited success with it. We also agreed that unless the caregiver is entirely in tune with the patient's thoughts, this system would be quite frustrating. My new computer with its speech files will completely eliminate the need for that board. However, if I get to the point where I am unable to move my head, then the letter board that Donna made could turn out to be the only option.

I am hoping that this computer will do for me everything that it is *supposed* to be able to do. If I had not stumbled on it, I never would have known it existed. No one at the ALS Association ever mentioned it. I have never seen anything about it in magazines, in newsletters, or articles about muscular dystrophy, etc. I've read all kinds of articles about equipment, but I have never seen this. My physical therapist is in awe.

My friend Gregg's mom died of ALS, and he is starry eyed at this. He keeps saying if his mom had access to this it would have had a major impact on her quality of life. (Gregg is a volunteer "buddy" provided for Linda through the MA chapter of the ALS Association. He visited Linda about once a week and helped with various tasks Linda needed done. He was also a good sounding board, as he went through this experience with his mom.)

Note: When Linda began this discussion about equipment, she made it clear that it was because she was proactive and did her own research that she became knowledgeable about what equipment was available. There are many people in her position

101

who do not have the will, know-how, or the resources to be as proactive as Linda was to advocate for themselves. Linda and I discussed this, and in an effort to help improve the lack of equipment information available to ALS patients, we decided that when Linda became an expert on the use of her new computer and the wheelchair adaptations, we would write an article together and submit it to local and national ALS publications. Hopefully, the article would provide powerful information to disabled people about some of the incredible technology that is available right now and can help them in their everyday lives.

Coincidentally, not too long after Linda and I had this discussion, she showed me a new book that she had just acquired. The book was Everyday Life with ALS: A Practical Guide, published by the ALS division of the MDA. This is an excellent book filled with very useful information about various kinds of equipment for daily living, mobility, exercise, transfers, and support. It also addresses home modifications, speech and communication, and respiratory issues. In addition, it lists many resources for the ALS patient and caregiver. This book was newly published in 2005. One can only hope that this wealth of crucial information is given to every single patient who is diagnosed with ALS. Such a book would have saved Linda countless hours of her time and energy researching information from every available resource to find equipment that might be appropriate for her progressing disabilities. Ironically, by the time Linda got this book, she already had most of the recommended equipment. However, we were both thrilled that finally, there was a superlative resource available for ALS patients and caregivers.

Chapter 18
Linda's Sister, Judy

Linda's sister, Judy, was very tentative about doing an interview to talk about Linda's life as a child. Judy kept insisting that she had few memories of herself and Linda together as children. There was a ten year age difference between the two of them. So, in fact, they did not spend a lot of time together when Linda was growing up. Judy remembers spending most of her summers away from her parents and with her maternal grandparents in NH. Her parents (and Linda) would often come up for family weekend visits.

Judy married very young (18), and once she was married and living in NH, she found that more time was spent with Linda. She and her husband John often would pick up Linda in Medford, MA, and bring her to NH to visit with them. After Judy had her daughter Susan, Linda spent even more time with them as she loved being with the baby. Linda was a terrific babysitter, and Susan loved the time she spent with her Aunt Linda.

When Linda herself got married, Judy believes that she and Linda became much closer. The two couples got along very well together and often exchanged visits to each other's homes.

Judy shares bits and pieces:

I do remember when Linda was born. It was a big deal to me because it was my dance recital! My mother wasn't there, and my father went out for a smoke when I was on the stage! So everybody in my family missed my dance recital, but Linda was worth it! I was very happy to be a big sister.

I thought Linda's birth meant I was going to have a baby to play with, but my mother had other ideas. She was very protective of her new little baby, and did everything herself. She would not let me play the little mother at all. Linda was, of course, cute and adorable and got lots of attention. However, my mom made sure she and I had our alone times, too. We'd go to the movies, shop together, or have dinner in Boston. Mom was attentive to all of us – Linda, my dad, and me.

When she was less than a year old, Linda contracted scarlet fever and got very, very ill. She almost died. In those days, people with scarlet fever were quarantined. My father had to move out. He was a milk man, and he certainly couldn't take the chance of carrying those germs around and infecting others. I think I stayed at home, however. We had a quarantine sign on the house to alert others. This went on for a few weeks, but then Linda bounced back and she was fine. However, it was a scary time.

I remember that when Linda was little, getting her to go to bed was always an issue. She was very headstrong, and she would refuse to go to bed. There was a show on TV that had some puppets, and she was scared to death of those puppets! So we'd just say to her, "The puppets are coming on the TV," and boom – she'd race to her room in a flash. She was about three years old at that time.

Linda took dancing lessons when she was young. She was pretty good at it, and enjoyed being on the stage. Linda was always dramatic – always dramatic! Sarah Heartburn we'd call her – always on center stage.

In the summertime when she was about five, she would get mad at her dolls, and she would open the back door and throw them out into the yard while saying, "Dirty rattlesnake skunk meat!" That was as close as she could get to swearing!

There were times when I was about twelve that I babysat for Linda, usually when my parents went grocery shopping or out to dinner. Linda and I would eat our supper and I would put her to bed. I loved that time with her. So I did get to play mom after all, about once a week, and it was great! She loved for me to read to her, and when she was a little older, we'd put on records and sing and dance together.

When Linda was about seven or eight, she had a friend named Margaret who was blind. They probably met in school. Linda was wonderful to this child and always looked out for her. Linda would make sure Margaret was included in everything she did. Oftentimes, Margaret came to play at our house and Linda would constantly mother her. Linda was always the mothering type.

Linda was really a good kid when she went to school, and she was always an excellent student and earned top grades. She enjoyed learning and education.

She never caused any trouble at school, but she sure gave my mother a good runaround! She and my mother went at it like hammer and nails. My dad was usually working or asleep, so Linda never butted heads with him. My mom never said, "Wait until your father gets home," if discipline had to be doled out. She took care of it, and Linda could be a little devil!

One time my grandparents came to visit, and when they walked in, Linda, who had just been disciplined, said with pride, "My mom hit me with the 'ardstick,' and she broke it!" Little Linda thought this was quite funny.

When she was little, she, my father, and I would go to the duck pond in Winchester and feed the ducks bread crusts. She loved animals, and feeding the ducks was a treat that the three of us would often do together. (It also gave my mom some time alone.)

We never went on long trips with our family, but we did do day trips – Linda loved going to the beach. We used to go on picnics at one of the state parks with our Aunt Helen and Uncle Jack, who were our godparents. We would always have a wonderful time. There were also many summer nights spent at Lynn Beach, where we'd have cookouts right on the beach.

As a kid, Linda was a typical little sister. She would get into my stuff and be annoying. My mother would try to take care of things like that, and Linda would usually acquiesce. We had separate bedrooms, and that helped.

When John and I started going together, Linda and I began to get closer. John and I took her places with us. After I had my daughter Susan, Linda would get on a bus and come up to visit for a few days. She was so good with Susan, and would play with her for hours. She was eleven or twelve by then. I always felt in a way it was too bad she didn't have children of her own.

One of the reasons I do not have a lot of memories of Linda as a kid is that I spent so much time away from my family and with my grandparents. When I was in the third grade, I went to CA with my grandmother for the whole winter. Of course, Linda was a baby then and it's one of the reasons my recollections of her as a baby are so vague. I wasn't around much.

I spent my summers in NH at the summer camp with my grandparents. My grandmother and I would be there during the week, and my grandfather would come up on weekends. Sometimes my parents and Linda would come up on the weekends along with my grandfather. One of the things Linda loved to do when she was up in the camp in NH was play with the cement ducks. She loved to water them with the hose all day long. My daughter Susan still has one of those very ducks!

At the camp there was a train that went by our back yard every morning at 8:20. We used to call it the "Getting Up Train" because we weren't supposed to be up before the train went by. Anyway, from the time she was very little, Linda was terrified of that train. Sometimes the adults would go out to wave as the conductor passed in the hopes of calming Linda's fears, but it never made any difference. She would still run and scream when it passed by.

The camp was on the lake. We had two boats there. The "Judy" boat was the motor boat, and the "Linda" boat was the little rowboat. We did lots of boating and swimming. We would water ski with the Judy boat, but that was not something Linda would ever do. That was too scary for her. She was really quite timid as a child.

Fortunately, she changed a lot when she got older. Going to Taiwan was a real turning point in her life. It was like she almost became a different person. She really grew up as a result of her experience there. She was such an emotional person before going to Taiwan, but that all changed. I am glad she went. She needed to get away and become her own person.

Before Linda and Jim were married, they often came up to the camp to visit us, and we had a lot of good times with them up there. In fact, the first time Linda introduced us to Jim was at camp. We had a cookout, and all the family was there – aunt and uncle, grandmother, parents. It was a good crowd, and poor Jim had never met any of them. I remember we were sitting at the picnic table – the kind that needs to have balanced seating. Well, somebody got up, the table tipped over, and my poor mother was on the ground, covered with potato salad and cheese and laughing to beat the band! My father yelled, "Are you all right?" which she was. John jumped up with his plate and never missed a beat – he just kept putting food on it! It was all quite hysterical, and Jim just took it all in. He was a good sport, and we liked him instantly.

(Leslie: I actually remember when Jim related this experience. He was quite impressed with Linda's family. He said if it had been his family, they would have been yelling and screaming over the mishap, certainly not laughing.)

Linda's wedding was small, but it was in a beautiful, big Episcopal cathedral in Brockton. My daughter Susan and Linda's friend Mary (also known as Betsy) were bridesmaids. Linda wore a very simple, pretty white dress. There were not many people there – mostly just close family members. After the wedding we went back to my parents' house for a little reception which was lovely. A woman who lived across the street was a caterer, so she brought in the food and a pretty cake. It was nice.

Linda and Jim came to the camp for their honeymoon. Before they arrived, we had gone over and pulled back the sheets and put pretty rose petals in the bed to make it a little fun for them. We decorated the place with candles, flowers, and left champagne, too!

Linda was especially close to my mother. They were very much alike in a lot of ways and they had a real connection. They did butt heads when she was little, but as adults they were extremely close. She was closer to my mother than to my father, and it was the opposite with me. Together, we were a very close and loving family. If one of us was hurt, we all hurt. If one of us was happy, we were all happy. We spent all the holidays and birthdays together. If we couldn't be together, we spoke to each other on the phone – frequently.

Because of our age difference, even though I was the older sister, I was more like a maternal figure to Linda. I don't think that really changed until she got married. From that time on we seemed more like peers, and our relationship evolved. As adults, we became a lot closer than when we were kids. We really weren't particularly close as kids because of the age difference.

Chapter 19
Another Diagnosis

You would think that having a devastating disease like ALS would be enough for any one person to handle. A routine mammogram in 2003 indicated that Linda had something else to worry about.

Linda:

My whole affair with breast cancer now seems so insignificant because I don't even remember when it was! I believe it was in 2003. I went to my primary care physician for a check up and had a routine mammogram, which presented something of concern. My previous mammogram had been about three years prior. I had not deliberately neglected myself, but up until that time, I did not think I could have a mammogram being wheelchair bound. However, the nurse practitioner said she thought they could accommodate me for a mammogram in my wheelchair, so they set up the appointment for me. That is the reason for the three year gap between mammograms. This cyst could have been there anytime within those three years.

I saw a surgeon who recommended a biopsy of a suspicious area in my right breast. I could see it very clearly on the films, but it was not palpable.

Lisa and I arranged for the biopsy procedure in November at the surgeon's office. Lisa accompanied me. It is not easy to be completely paralyzed and deal with this kind of procedure. It was done in my wheelchair. They wheeled me up to a mammogram type machine, propped me up, held me up (all while I am still in my chair) and located the area in question. Then they performed the biopsy. The most difficult part of this was that my right arm needed to be elevated above my head. A normal person would have stretched up the arm and held onto a handle above the machine. I however, don't hold onto anything! So Miss Lisa held my arm up in the air for quite awhile. The whole procedure took at least 20 minutes which is a long time to hold something up. At that time, I still had some control over my right hand, but that control was going very quickly. I knew this because with each successive loss there had been twitching and uncontrollable muscle spasms. That day my arm was jumping like the Energizer bunny! My shoulder was also jumping, and of course, as they were performing this medical procedure, they wanted me to be still. Lisa was trying to keep my parts from moving.

For this biopsy they made some kind of small incision and took some tissue samples. The tool they used looked like a fat magic marker and it felt like a punch hole being inserted into my breast. They drew out threads of tissue that Lisa said looked like strands of spaghetti. Anyway, we got through it, and within 24 hours, I got a phone call informing me that the biopsy showed cancer. So I made another appointment with the surgeon, Dr. Suniti Nimbkar, who is associated with Brigham and Women's Hospital.

Dr. Nimbkar explained that it was cancer, but at this point it was not invasive and had not spread outside of this area. I always questioned how they could know this just from the biopsy. I do not remember the word she used to describe this kind of cancer, but she did say that at this point, what was there was not threatening other areas. However, left to itself, it could change and become very aggressive. They strongly advised surgery. The doctor said the treatment for this would be a lumpectomy. For normal people, that would be followed up by radiation. In my case, radiation has many risks, so she felt the only option was to cut it out and hope for the best. My concern with the idea of a surgical lumpectomy was that having ALS, if I went under general anesthesia and needed to be put on a ventilator, I would never, ever get off. I will not go on a vent with this disease. I am adamant about this.

I expressed my concern to Dr. Nimbkar. She was very knowledgeable about ALS. I have a feeling that she probably studied up on it before talking with me. She assured me that this surgery could be done under local anesthesia. She knew an

110

anesthesiologist who was very familiar with ALS issues because the anesthesiologist's mother had died from ALS. Dr. Nimbkar said she would contact Dr. Liz Eldridge and approach her about working on the surgery.

The next thing I knew Dr. Eldridge called me to tell me that she would like to come here, to my home, and meet with me to assess the entire situation. She did so on her day off. I thought she was amazing. She was here for over two hours and was very personable. She fully assessed all my issues, including my breathing. She assured me she was confident we could do this under a local, and she would have a back-up anesthesia available. The back-up was something she liked to call "Milk of Amnesia," which she would administer through a mask if the pain became too unbearable. I told her about Lisa, and how she had been with me through the biopsy, and that Dr. Nimbkar had asked Lisa if she would be willing to accompany me and come into the OR. *The doctor* invited Lisa – it was not my idea. Dr. Eldridge was in complete agreement with that. While Dr. Eldridge was here, I also mentioned my DNR (**D**o **N**ot **R**esuscitate order) to her. After our meeting, everything was set up for the surgery.

A couple of days prior to the surgery, I met another anesthesiologist at the hospital. I said something about making sure there was reference to my DNR request on my paper work. He said it wouldn't matter. He said that in a surgical situation if anything goes wrong, even if you have a DNR, they ignore it. I never knew this, and I said I could not go through the surgery knowing that. He asked if I had discussed this with Dr. Eldridge and Dr. Nimbkar. I said I hadn't because I did not know about it. He told me to discuss it with them.

I called Dr. Eldridge and I told her my concern. I asked her if I wrote up a contract that she was not to go against my DNR, pre, during, or post surgically, would she sign it and would she stick by it. She did not hesitate and said yes. I then approached Dr. Nimbkar with the same information, and she too agreed. Dr. Eldridge made a special visit to my home to sign the agreement. Lisa hand delivered the agreement to Dr. Nimbkar's office. Neither of them had a problem with this. It released them from any liability and it complied with my wishes.

At the South Shore Hospital we had a very easy experience because Noel, Lisa's mom, used to be the manager of the radiology department, and the name Constantino, opened doors. Everywhere we went, the minute Lisa introduced herself, everything was expedited.

First we went to radiology for a procedure similar to a mammogram. Once again Lisa exposed herself to radiation while she stood by me and helped hold my arm up and steady my body while they located the cancer. They inserted needles into my breast to "map" the area for the surgeon. That was a pretty uncomfortable procedure but less so than the biopsy had been. Following the mapping, we moved, needles protruding from my breast and all, to pre-op. Dr. Eldridge came in to start my IV herself and made sure I was comfortable while we waited for our place in the OR.

About an hour later, we went into surgery. Lisa was wearing her scrubs, cap, and slippers! I drove myself into the OR, under my own power, wide awake, and they transferred me to the table. Dr. Eldridge knew what was required for positioning so I could breathe, and she worked with me and the surgeon to get me comfortable, while still allowing the surgeon to work. The surgery went very well.

After the local anesthesia was given to me, I did experience a slight period of breathing stress during which Lisa jumped in and used her special technique that helped me clear my throat and breathe more easily. The OR staff was impressed! I was good... up to a point, and then it hurt. About half way through the surgery I felt severe pain. They could not give me more local anesthesia. The minute I flinched, Dr. Eldridge said, "It's time for me to help," but I said, "No, I'm okay." She said, "No, it's not worth it." It was time for Milk of Amnesia! I breathed it in through a face mask. Under this anesthesia I could hear everything, but I was in a twilight zone.

112

All through the surgery, Lisa sat to my left, right beside the table. The OR nurses literally had to walk around her. *(Linda became VERY emotional at this point as she described Lisa's role in her surgery.)* I can't believe she did that. She was holding my arm. I still cannot believe anyone would do that for me. She was right there. She did much more than provide moral support. She acted as my interpreter and anticipated my needs so I didn't need to verbalize them. Her presence was invaluable to the doctors and the entire OR staff and they thanked her as they would have any colleague. Later, in a letter written on Lisa's behalf, Dr. Eldridge described Lisa as having functioned as my appendage throughout! I know I could never have gone through that operation, physically or emotionally without Lisa and I can never truly thank her adequately.

Afterwards, Lisa told me what I was babbling on about under the "Milk of Amnesia," but now I can't remember. My babbling had to do with what I heard them all saying at the time. Apparently I was contributing to the conversation, but made no sense! I have never had any kind of anesthesia like that. It really was like being in the twilight zone.

The surgery was completed with no further pain, and as soon as it was over and they removed the anesthesia, I was *instantly* back in the real world – no drugged feeling, no disorientation. Lisa said it was like someone had flicked a switch. I went from babbling to immediate coherence mid-sentence. They said it was over, and of course I started to cry. Lisa told them it was because I was happy it was all over.

After the operation, they lifted me off the table and sat me back in my power wheelchair. I drove myself to the recovery room. I was covered in blood and antiseptic and must have been quite a sight rolling along the corridors!

That afternoon I went home. Lisa stayed with me for a couple of nights. I had limited discomfort. I took Tylenol, nothing stronger – no Percocet or anything similar. I think that night Noel brought over lobster salad and we drowned our sorrows in dinner! It had been an extremely long day.

Dr. Nimbkar said at the follow up that she wished they had taken a larger margin around the area for safety. When you are cutting out a cancer of this sort, there is no flashing sign saying, "Cut here." She did the best she could, but after the fact, she wished she had taken more. *(Later tests revealed that some cancer cells still remained.)*

I met with a follow up oncologist – Dr. Rolf Freter, also at South Shore Hospital. We discussed what I should do now. Normally they would recommend six weeks of radiation. For me, even transporting me to the hospital and then moving me onto a table for treatment are prohibitive. Also, radiation can have side effects – breathing and pneumonia issues, and the doctors were concerned. Another option was oral chemotherapy. However, both of the two drugs they would normally use for this particular cancer carry side effects of blood clots. For me, blood clots are a high risk anyway because I am immobile. The oncologist did not recommend that course. He was very open. He said he would do whatever I wanted. I expressed that I truly believed I was more at risk from ALS than I was from this slow growing cancer that hopefully, had been removed completely. Thus, we decided to just follow up on a semi-annual basis and hope for the best.

It is very interesting that to me that in another life, the news of breast cancer would have devastated me. From my perspective with ALS, the breast cancer is just another inconvenience, another bump in the road that I dealt with in the best manner I could. Upon hearing the whole story after the fact, my neurologist was very glad that I had stopped treatment after the surgery.

Note: Linda met with the oncologist every six months for follow-up exams. There were no significant changes and she did not have any additional treatments.

Chapter 20
The Big Trip

In the early days of Linda's illness, when she was no longer mobile enough to get into someone's car to go someplace, Linda would call Bill's Taxi, a local company which also provided van transport for wheelchairs. This was expensive, so Linda utilized this option judiciously. She did schedule the van transport when she had appointments at the Lahey clinic, and every once in awhile, along with a buddy, she would treat herself to a shopping trip to the nearby TJ Maxx or Wal-Mart. One time she rented the van so that she, my husband Norm, and I could go on an outing to Nantasket beach. Once there, we walked with Linda (in her wheelchair) along the pavement near the shore, inhaling the glorious salty air. Linda loved the ocean, and having the opportunity to mosey along the beach and watch the crashing waves invigorated her and renewed her spirits. After about a half hour's leisurely stroll, we went across the street to a restaurant that was handicap accessible. The restaurant was on the second floor, and had a great view of the water. We were fortunate enough to get a seat by the window. Linda was in heaven! After a delicious lunch, during which we were entertained by parasailers (!), we boarded the van for the return trip to Linda's condo. Considering the fact that Linda rarely got to go beyond the restricting walls of her condo, this was a very special treat for her. She truly appreciated outings like this because she never knew if, or when, she'd have an opportunity for another.

When Linda and Lisa discovered the wheelchair loaner program from Compassionate Care, it opened up a whole new world for Linda. Lisa and Linda could borrow the van for up to a week at a time, and when they did, it was a whirlwind week! Each day they would plan a different outing – Plymouth, Newport, the doctor, the dentist, the mall, the homes of friends. The Compassionate Care van was an absolute godsend, and it had a huge impact on Linda's quality of life. The van made her feel "almost normal," as she could travel to many places and be like everyone else.

In June of 2005, after intensive planning and organization, Lisa and Linda set out for a very ambitious adventure – a three-day stay at Linda's sister Judy's house in New Hampshire. This chapter details all the excitement, trials, and tribulations of the trip.

Linda:
Prelude

When I was first diagnosed, my sister and brother-in-law were about to build a new home and without telling me, they built that home with a handicap ramp and a walk-in shower. They did it with the idea that I would probably end up living with them. When my sister suggested it my brother-in-law never ever questioned it in any way. He was in 100% agreement. Down the road we all realized it would not be in my - or their - best interests to live together. However, that ramp and that bathroom made it possible for me to visit them frequently in the early stages of my disease. Now, with access to the wheelchair van and with Lisa's willingness to drive, I have been able to visit again. Without those accommodations, I never would be able to visit their home. To this very day, I am enjoying occasional visits to their home.

When you are handicapped it's pretty rare that you can visit anyone in their home because most homes are not handicap accessible. I will be forever grateful that my sister and brother-in-law made their home accessible for me. My sister's house is set up so that the ramp runs along the back of her house up onto the deck. My brother-in-law has built a couple of wedge-type ramps to bridge the one step from the deck into the house. I've never had any problem getting in there. It is a fantastic thing to be able to visit my family. I can never express adequately my appreciation that they made all those accommodations for me.

I did have another friend, Amanda, who had a home that was handicap accessible because she had a disabled aunt who lived

116

with them. A couple of years ago she invited me to a cookout. She is a wonderful pianist and we went in the house and into her music room. She played for us on the grand piano. It was so great to be able to go into someone else's home.

When Lisa and I are out in the van, if we drive by a home that is handicap accessible, we will often remark that, "We ought to drop in!"

It is amazing the lengths to which some of my friends have gone to accommodate me at their homes. Two years in a row Gail prepared beautiful outdoor garden parties. Though I could not go into the house, I was able to have a delightful backyard visit and enjoy the party with all the guests.

The prize should probably go to Barbara and Mike who invited me, Lisa, Lisa's daughter, and Gail to their home for what we thought was going to be a cookout on the lawn. When we arrived, it was apparent they had an extreme makeover in their garage. Everything had been cleared out of the garage. For this occasion, Mike had built stairs and put a storage floor on the rafters for everything that had been in the garage with the exception of Mike's collectible, million dollar Mustang. They had candles burning on all of those stairs. They brought in shrubbery from outside, and set up a banquet table with beautiful linens, fine China, and candles burning everywhere. Mike's tool bench had been converted into a serving buffet. It was absolutely gorgeous, and we enjoyed a wonderful evening. It's amazing what some people can do to make you feel "normal" and enjoy the things everyone else does.

The Big Trip
In early June, 2005, my PCA and friend, Lisa, and I took on the adventure of a lifetime. I put us right up there with Admiral Byrd, or any great explorer, or anyone trying to climb Mount Everest, because we overcame great obstacles to achieve our goal. We went to NH to visit my sister and brother-in-law.

This trip took a lot of intricate planning. We had to measure the distance of my bed from the floor, then have my sister do the same for her guest room bed. We had to know that my lift equipment would be compatible in her home. That being figured out, all things looked like a go. We were optimistic we could stay two nights, but if breathing became too much of an issue after one night, we'd leave. We were hoping for the best.

While we were here making our plans about what to bring, my sister was busy trying to move some things out of her guest room to make more space for my equipment. I applaud her for her forethought. Many people never would have considered that.

We left on a Wednesday morning. Shauna, came over in the morning and got me ready. When Lisa showed up, Shauna was prepared to help pack the van. Lisa had driven to Falmouth the previous day to pick up the Compassionate Care van, which we could keep for the week. What we had to bring was… everything! Everything from equipment to rubber gloves. Lisa had to dismantle the pivot lift in order to get it in the van, and that thing weighs about 75 or more pounds, so moving it into the van was challenging. We had to take the commode chair and the frame that fits in the shower. We had to take my pillows and a large, foam wedge. We were hoping with that foam, my pillows, and a back rest from Lisa's mother, we would be able to adapt a conventional bed to approximate my mechanical bed for sleeping positioning. We had all my personal items, toiletries, etc., and the board with the bar that goes on my bed at night, and some minor items such as clothing to wear!

Lisa and Shauna moved everything out onto the sidewalk, and piled it up next to the van as they tried to figure out how to pack it in. I went out in my wheelchair, and we realized that this was a great photo opportunity. The mailman had just arrived and we coerced him into taking a photo of all of us and all of the things from my house. He said, "Are you going camping?" We laughed, and told him we were going on a home visit. His comment was that he always thought that when you take more than half the contents of your home with you, you are either moving or going camping! Ultimately we got the van all packed, said good bye to Shauna, and Lisa and I were on the road at 11:06 AM. We had hoped to be off by 11:00, so we thought we had done well. First stop was in Peabody at the Puritan Lawn Memorial Park Cemetery where my parents and grandparents were laid to rest. Lisa had read my mind and knew that I would like to do that, even though I hadn't mentioned it. The previous day she had purchased some flowering plants for us to leave at the graves. We paid our respects at the cemetery, then got back into the van and continued to our destination of Milton, NH.

My sister greeted us when we arrived, and we relaxed with a snack on her screened-in porch for a short while. Then my brother-in-law John and his grandson Chris arrived, and they proceeded to help Lisa unpack the van and get everything into the house. I cannot use a bathroom until my equipment is available. Around dinner time my niece and her husband, their daughter and her boyfriend, two cousins whom I had not seen since the Cliff Walk, plus another couple and another friend from the area whom I have known for years all arrived. We had a Chinese food feast followed by a birthday cake for me. It was a little belated birthday party because I had not seen any of them at the time of my birthday. It was all very, very enjoyable. We took a break to move to the back porch to watch the evening visit from the wild deer who gather in the field behind my sister's house every night at 7:15. It is very interesting... they do not come at 7:14, they come at exactly 7:15!

During the visit, everyone was looking at the scrapbook that Leslie had completed for me. The scrapbook is a celebratory pictorial history of my life with ALS. Everyone loved it! We finally got to bed around midnight. That was interesting because though we had brought all my equipment, it was still challenging to put me in the antique sleigh bed with a footboard, dust ruffle, and side frame as opposed to my adjustable bed at home that has no footboard, no sideboard, etc. Eventually I was in bed and I slept pretty well. Lisa slept on an Aero bed in the living room. The big challenge was turning off the chimes in my sister's huge grandfather clock, but we managed to get that under control. I think everyone got some sleep.

Thursday morning we got up and Lisa got me into the bathroom for my morning routine, which takes about two hours. The guest room has a walk-in shower, so my equipment was fine in the bathroom. One thing that was challenging... the carpeting in the guest room was quite plush, a very deep pile, and Lisa had a hard time trying to move the pivot lift on that. The very first night she hurt her shoulder trying to move it, and she was in quite a bit of discomfort. It made us really appreciate the indoor-outdoor commercial-type carpeting in my condo. After we had showered and dressed, my sister made a lovely brunch and then Judy, John, Lisa, and I took off for Maine. We visited York Beach, Ogunquit, Wells, and Kennebunkport. It was hot, sunny, and beautiful. I wanted to eat at the Maine Diner in Wells because I see it on TV all the time. We had an early dinner there, and we got back to my sister's house in time to see the deer at 7:15!

Afterward, my niece Susan, her husband Bernie, and their son Chris came over and we watched home movies from ancient history. It was quite entertaining. We had so many laughs. There were films of me when I was about 12, and Susan when she was little, and me ice skating with my Uncle Ed when I was about 17 or 18. My nephew said I looked like Laverne of Laverne and Shirley! There were lots of fond memories of holidays and birthdays. How great it was to see my parents and to see how young they looked. It was moving and funny.

Ultimately, everyone went home, the house settled down, and once again we got to bed about midnight. Friday would be our final day of vacation. Judy made another elaborate country breakfast-brunch. I battled it out with the buckwheat pancakes! Finally about noon, Lisa and I got on the road to go to Vermont. We invited my sister to come along, but she declined. John was working. On the way we drove by Lake Winnipesauke in NH. It was motorcycle rally week at Laconia and Weir's beach, so we took a little detour to see the sites, which Lisa very much enjoyed because she is a motorcycle aficionado.

Eventually we got to Newbury, VT at about 3:30 in the afternoon. Newbury is where I spent so many wonderful times in the past at a bed and breakfast that is no longer in operation. We stopped at my friend Pat Smith's house, but she was not home. (Pat had owned the B&B.) So we traveled a little further to one of my old haunts, the P&H Truck Stop. We enjoyed a terrific Truck Stop meal, then headed back through Newbury and once again went to Pat's house. She was now home and was flabbergasted that we were there! We had a little visit in her driveway. Lisa took a tour of the house, but I could not get in. It had been three or four years since I last saw Pat. The black flies were voracious, and after about a half hour, they won the battle, and we said goodbye.

We arrived back at Milton at about 9 PM. My first order of business was to use the bathroom! I said to Lisa, that I didn't know how I did it. I had gone nine hours without a bathroom break. I think I should be in the Guinness book! My niece, her husband, and her son, came back over to help Lisa pack the van. My sister tried to prevail upon us to stay one more night, but getting ready in the morning is two hours minimum, another 30 – 60 minutes to pack, and Lisa felt she would rather leave Friday night. We had the help to pack the van and it was late enough that we should not have any traffic going home. We left at 10 PM and ran into some heavy, heavy downpours, but they were temporary. When we got to the part of the highway where we had to choose whether to go on route 128 around Boston as we always do or go through Boston, we decided that it was late at night and there would not be any traffic, and since Boston was more direct, we would take that route. WRONG!!! When we got to the tunnel, it was closed for repairs. We were detoured all over creation: by the Fleet Center, through Chinatown, through the North End. It was a very circuitous route in bumper-to-bumper traffic.

At long last we got on the South East Expressway and we finally reached Rockland at about 1:30 AM. Normally we should have been home by midnight. The weather conditions and the detour had added about an hour and a half to our trip. When we got home, Lisa was alone and had to take care of all the equipment – no easy task. She had to reassemble the lift in order to be able to use it to get me to bed. She left here well after 2 AM.

121

It was an amazing trip. I did everything I wanted to do. I know in my heart that I will never see Newbury, Vermont again, and it was very important for me to reminisce. I think that it was a really good visit with my family. I know that my sister greatly enjoyed it, and I know that it broadened her awareness of what living with ALS really means. I also know that no one, *absolutely no one* in my life could have undertaken what Lisa did. No one else had the ability and the courage to achieve such a challenge. And... she made it look easy!

One postscript – when we got home and Lisa tried to move me on my rug, it was like - whoosh – so easy!

The exhilaration of this venture was incomparable. It was quite a feeling...so magnificent and wonderful. I felt like I was on a world tour, and I *almost* could forget I had ALS.

Chapter 21
Breathing

Linda:

One of the big issues with ALS is breathing and choking or rather, not being able to breathe and choking. People do not realize that ultimately, that is what kills many with ALS. Most people are very aware of the external effects, so they know that the ALS person cannot move or walk, but they do not think about the fact that muscles are also in your chest, lungs, and throat. ALS destroys those muscles as well.

My breathing issues all started within the past year, in 2004. Part of it is evidenced by the slowness with which I talk because I cannot get enough air to speak normally. My voice is straining when I talk without the chatterbox microphone. (*This is a device which increases the volume of Linda's voice. She seldom used it.*) I move when I talk because I am trying to force enough air out of my lungs to speak.

Recently the Muscular Dystrophy Association published an excellent article about breathing and choking and what could be done to help. In general, there can be multiple causes for choking. Usually they're unrelated to eating or drinking. However, sometimes food will cause choking. Last weekend when I was at my sister's, I had a very hard time eating buckwheat pancakes. The texture triggered the coughing and choking reflex. I have trouble with anything whole grain – whole wheat bread, brown rice, anything of the whole grain texture. One day Lisa made French toast with whole wheat bread. Tasted fine, but every bite would set me off with a series of coughing spasms. Another thing with ALS is, once a coughing reflex is triggered, it's almost impossible to quiet it down. It's a reflex out of control, so I have learned that certain foods are problematic, and I do try to stay away from them.

However, I never thought a thing about the buckwheat pancakes until I started eating them and reacted. It was kind of like trying to swallow gravel.

(Note: Almost immediately after Linda and Lisa left Judy's house in NH after their three day visit, Judy called me in a panic. She was horrified after seeing Linda's choking episode. Though Lisa was able to mediate the situation and Linda was okay, it scared Judy to death. Having seen this, she was now very concerned about Linda continuing to live alone when choking was such a dangerous reality in her life. I agreed with Judy that it must have been very frightening to watch Linda suffer through such an ordeal. Though I told her I certainly understood her concerns about Linda living alone, I knew that Linda was not even remotely ready to give up her independence for a nursing home. I tried to reassure Judy there was constant traffic in her condo all day long – either the PCAs who were there several times daily, or various friends. However, I am quite sure nothing I said made Judy feel any better. While she was thrilled that Linda and Lisa were able to visit for a few days, her latest perception of living with ALS was most distressing.)

Most people with ALS will find themselves choking out of the blue for no reason. Sometimes I will just inhale a breath, and that's all it takes to get me started, literally choking on air. My sister keeps asking if oxygen will help, but it will not help. I have found that an over the counter drug called Mucinex, which was recommended by my specialist, does help me to cough up secretions to a certain extent. It keeps them thin enough for me to be able to handle, but it's still a big struggle.

An article in the MDA newsletter explained something that I have been aware of for quite awhile – strong odors can set off a choking reaction. Recently at my birthday, I received bouquet after bouquet of fresh cut flowers. One bouquet had a very fragrant lily included. It had me coughing so uncontrollably that we ended up putting it outside on the back deck. At my sister's house, she has fragrant candles everywhere, and the morning I was struggling with the pancakes, she had been burning an apple pie scented candle. She did put it out, but by then, the reaction had begun, and there is no turning back. I have to be very careful of scented body lotions, shower soap, etc. I do not try to get everything unscented however, because they do not all set me off – just certain ones. Scented candles, even if they are unlit, just put me right over the edge. I first became aware of my hyper-sensitivity to scents first thing in the morning when my health aides would toilet me, and the scent of my own urine would get me coughing uncontrollably. So now they all know to flush right away.

The effort it takes to cough and clear my lungs, is often more effort than I am able to expend. Lisa sometimes will do a technique on me just for the heck of it where I will breathe in as deeply as I can, and as I exhale, she will push on my chest, and that helps me empty my lungs. Then the next breath will fill them to a greater extent. I don't know right now what my breathing capacity is. The last time I had it checked was more than two years ago, and then, if I recall, it was about 70%. I am sure it is now well below that.

There's a choice that each individual has to make – whether or not they will breathe on their own until the disease puts an end to that, or whether they will go on a vent, which can definitely extend your life, but there are quality of life issues. For me, I am far too much of a control freak to deal with going on a vent. Awhile ago Lisa and I visited a gentleman named Ed who lives in a residential facility. He has ALS and is on a vent. I wanted to observe him because I was already thinking ahead and struggling with the whole issue. So we visited Ed and part way through the visit, his vent began to malfunction, as they sometimes can. His wife, Donna, immediately told one aide to get another aide, a specific person who knew how to correct the problem. The aide came back with a different person who did not know what to do. Donna was starting to get very frightened for her husband and was demanding that they find the specified aide who knew how to handle this emergency. Meanwhile Lisa and I were observing Ed unable to get air, starting to change color, trying not to panic. Finally the requested aide showed up, took control of the potentially deadly situation, and proceeded to chastise the other aide, asking him why he did not find him immediately. In those two minutes, that man almost died, and I saw the panic in his eyes. I saw the panic in his wife's eyes. When we left there I said to Lisa, "Now I know I can never, never put myself in that situation." I would live in terror every minute of my life, knowing that at any moment that could happen, and the "professional" person taking care of me might not know what to do. It is another personal decision. Ron Hoffman (of Compassionate Care) knows that I have decided not to go on a vent. He personally agrees with me on that. However, he has told me that he knows ALS patients who have chosen to go on a vent who never regretted it. He's also known people who have gone on a vent and have regretted the decision. Once a person with ALS is put on a vent, there is no weaning off. You would be on it forever, and it's not what I want to do.

~~~~~~~~~~~~~~~~~~~~~~~~~~~~

Lisa's recollections on the machines they obtained to help with breathing/coughing issues:
Sometime in the summer of 2005, Linda agreed to get more equipment to assist with her breathing. We discussed this with Dr. Russell and he provided options for various equipment we could obtain. Typically, Linda looked into it, thought about it, then decided what we would get. We had tried things like different cough syrups and such to loosen the phlegm in her chest. We discovered that food often triggered the congestion. Linda was having more and more difficulty trying to clear the congestion on her own. I would help her cough, but that was another obstacle – just getting Linda to let me assist her. She was very independent, and would try repeatedly to clear her throat, but often to no avail. I explained to her that with my quad patient in CA, we did a "quad cough," which is similar to a Heimlich maneuver. She ultimately allowed me to push on her chest to help her expel the congestion. She was losing the accessory muscles that go around the ribs that we use in our breathing regularly. Those muscles were deteriorating so she didn't have the force she needed to cough. Her diaphragm was also getting weaker which compounded the difficulty. Her breathing had become a lot more shallow by this time, so she was not moving excretions regularly. From that point, when necessary, I manually pushed on her chest to clear it, and

sometimes I would take a tissue and run it through the back of her mouth to pull out the phlegm that came up. I would often get a handful of phlegm like that. Sometimes she was able to cough it up, but more often than not, I would push on her chest and have that tissue ready to get it all out.

She did get the equipment – a suctioning machine and a cough assist machine. The cough assist forced air into the lungs and immediately pulled it back out, essentially inducing a cough. We had read about it in ALS brochures, so we knew it was equipment that some ALS patients used. Both of these pieces of equipment sat in Linda's cabinet for awhile before we attempted to utilize them. As Linda's congestion progressed and I was starting to do the manual cough, I somehow talked her into *at least trying* the new equipment. Linda agreed that she would allow me to use it on her, and when we were comfortable with it, then I could teach the other aides.

We started with the cough assist machine. At first it didn't seem to do anything. There were different pressures you could change, and you could regulate how much air went in and how much came out. We experimented with that. Later, a respiratory therapist from the company came out and showed me how the equipment worked. The suctioning equipment I was more familiar with because I had used that in the past, but the cough assist was new to me. After he demonstrated the proper way to use the equipment, Linda and I practiced. I got her to start using it in the evenings at bedtime. This was the optimal time for her because she would have trouble sleeping because of the phlegm build up, and she would spend half her nights trying to cough stuff up. Once we got into the rhythm of doing the cough assist machine, and doing it before bedtime, she realized she was sleeping better. She would still wake up in the morning with congestion, but she started off the night congestion free.

I was still dragging a lot of her secretions out by hand, and so she finally relented to try the suction machine, but that scared her. It is not easy to let someone stick something down your throat. I was concerned about gagging her, but she would say, "Don't worry if it gags me!" She was actually pretty brave about it, and we did start to use it. However, she would only use either of the machines when I was there, and there were plenty of shifts when I wasn't there. Though we did demonstrate the machines to a couple of the aides, Linda did not feel really comfortable with having them use the equipment on her. The two of us got good at it though, and managed to keep her airway clear for much of the time when we used it.

Chapter 22
Morning and Evening Routines

Linda's social life did not end with ALS. If anything, it got even busier. Friends were constantly dropping by to visit, chat, and get caught up on the latest happenings. The majority of these visits were unannounced and spontaneous. Most of Linda's friends felt there was no need to call because Linda would surely be home. Linda's front door was always left unlocked after the morning health care worker came so that friends could walk into the condo easily.

When company arrived, they would almost always find Linda in her living room, fully dressed and sitting in her wheelchair reading or occasionally watching TV. Few visitors ever realized what an arduous and lengthy ordeal it was for Linda to get out of bed, get washed and dressed and into her wheelchair for the day. Then she would have to repeat a similar routine to go to bed at night. It would have been so much easier just to stay in bed each day. But Linda did not do "easy." She was adamant about getting out of that bed, showering, and dressing <u>every</u> <u>single</u> <u>day</u>. It was another example that conveyed a sense of normalcy, and she was determined to continue with her morning and evening routines for as long as she possibly could.

After Linda and I had been working on her book for several months, I told her that I would like to come over and observe a morning and an evening ritual so I could chronicle these experiences in the book. She agreed. Though Linda had a number of different PCAs who got her up in the morning and put her to bed at night, we decided it would make more sense for me to come at times when Lisa was on duty, as she was the most skilled and experienced.

Though I actually observed the evening routine two months before I observed the morning one, I will begin with the morning ritual. The pictures I took at both sessions will also illuminate the use of some of her specialized equipment.

Linda's Morning Routine
Observed Sunday, September 4, 2005

Lisa arrived about 8:15, though she was scheduled to get Linda up at 8:30. I was supposed to be there at 8:30 to observe, but I got there early, too – at 8:20. Linda was in bed, and was sipping a glass of water Lisa had brought her. Next to Linda's head on the pillow was a round disc, about four inches in diameter. It was the Lifeline. She had gotten this new Lifeline a few weeks prior. With this disc pinned to her pillow, she could summon the Lifeline if she needed it by tapping it with her head. (She could no longer manage the hand-operated Lifeline.)

Lisa began exercising Linda's arms, stretching them over her head individually, about eight times each, then together. Then she started stretching Linda's legs, bending each at the knee, then straight up. Normally, Lisa stretches each leg out to the side, as well, but Linda's left leg was still quite sore from a fall two weeks before. After the morning stretches, Lisa transferred Linda to the pivot lift, then her sliding shower chair, and rolled her into the bathroom, where Linda took care of her morning business. While Linda was on the toilet, Lisa unplugged the wheelchair (which gets charged every night), stowed the electrical cord in back of the chair, and massaged the new gel seat to ready it for another day. That finished, Lisa brushed Linda's teeth, and brushed her hair with a scalp massage.

Linda told Lisa what she wanted to wear for the day, and Lisa brought Linda's clothes into the bathroom. Then Lisa slid Linda's chair into the shower. Lisa, who changed her clothes, got into the shower as well and began by washing Linda's hair. She used a hand hose, which is a necessity. She then cleaned and rinsed Linda, moved her out of the shower, and got her dressed. She brought Linda back to the bedroom, transferred her to the pivot lift, pulled up her undies and pants, and then transferred her to the wheelchair. She attached the leg rests, made Linda comfy, and the job was done. This entire routine took about 90 minutes. (Lisa is speedier in this process than most of the other PCAs.)

While Lisa was still at Linda's, Linda requested that Lisa use the cough assist machine on her, as she felt she needed to clear her lungs. After a few minutes Linda said she felt better and the machine had given her some relief.

Observation of Linda's Bedtime Routine
Tuesday, July 5, 2005

Lisa was going to be on duty for this night, which I wanted to observe. She was not scheduled to arrive until 10:30 PM, so I told Linda I would come with dinner around 6:00, and we would spend some time together before Lisa's arrival. I arrived at 6:00, but Mary Beth (another PCA) was still taking care of Linda, so I waited for about 15 minutes until Mary Beth finished.

Linda had been in bed for most of the day because her power wheelchair had died a few days before. With the wheelchair out of commission, it was extremely uncomfortable for Linda. For one thing, there was the risk of getting blood clots when sitting in one position for too long. Linda was unable to move her body in the non-electric chair on her own. In addition, she could get bedsores very easily from sitting in the same position for a great length of time. Obviously, a power wheelchair in good working order was not a luxury, but an everyday necessity for Linda.

The wheelchair "specialist" had been out to Linda's earlier in the day to fix the chair, but he could not, nor did he know when they would be able to come and get her chair to take it in to get fixed. Once again, she would have to cope with a "loaner" which did not have all the bells and whistles of her Cadillac.

In addition to her wheelchair being on the fritz, her computer was as well. The new computer had been out of order more times than it had been working.

131

Before eating, Linda and I reviewed my notes from our last interview session, made the necessary edits, then moved on to dinner. We enjoyed chicken and pasta salad left over from my July 4th barbeque. Then we chatted away for most of the remaining time. I made some more entries into Linda's new address book. Lisa made her entrance at her appointed time.

Lisa had bought a new brush for Linda, and she immediately began brushing Linda's hair with it so as to massage her scalp. This was one of the bedtime rituals. Before moving into the bedroom, Lisa gave Linda a couple of Coricidin (which she got down with Cool Whip on a teaspoon). This helped relieve her congestion at night. Lisa then moved the wheelchair into the bedroom to prepare for the transfer into the pivot lift. Once in the pivot lift, Lisa wheeled Linda over to the rolling commode chair (also known as the sliding shower chair) for the transfer. Linda's transfer into the pivot lift and from the lift to the commode chair was simple and routine with Lisa. Once she was transferred, Lisa wheeled Linda into the bathroom to do her business.

While Linda was occupied, I asked Lisa to transfer me from the wheelchair to the lift. I wanted to experience what it felt like. Lisa easily had me out of the chair and into the lift. While in the lift, I did feel secure, though strange, to be in such an awkward position. Lisa transferred me right onto the bed. It seemed very easy and not at all intimidating for the transferee.

After Linda had taken care of her business, Lisa returned to the bathroom to clean her up, brush her teeth, wash her face and hands, brush her hair again for a good head massage, and change her into a night shirt and fresh undies. She also applied some cream to Linda's finger nails. The cream was prescribed by a doctor to eliminate some kind of nail infection she had that gave her nails white streaky marks. The cream was obviously working because the marks were disappearing. Lisa then rolled Linda back to the bedroom and proceeded to transfer her to the bed. To do this, Lisa had all the pillows propped up in the middle of the bed on the left side. She brought the lift (or actually *I* did!) up against the middle of the right side of the bed. Then Lisa made the transfer, and there

132

was Linda, sitting on the side of the bed, propped up by the pillows. Next, Lisa laid her down on her back with her legs extending to the foot of the bed. Lisa grasped Linda's feet and pushed her body all the way up to the headboard. She was very careful not to hit Linda's head on the headboard. The pillows were then put next to Linda and under her head.

Lisa adjusted the bed so that Linda's back was elevated about 20 degrees and her feet were elevated as well at about the same angle. This was how Linda had to sleep to avoid choking on her congestion. Lisa removed Linda's support hosiery and massaged her feet and legs with lotion.

On occasion in the past, Linda wore a device on each hand that she and Lisa had created to prevent her fingers from curling up. They put a stiff piece of cardboard inside a slipper sock, then cut a hole near the bottom for Linda's hand to fit through. Her hand was secured in place with a wide elasticized band resting atop a piece of foam laid across the back of Linda's hand. Linda was convinced that wearing this device on a regular basis for awhile had kept her fingers from curling. In fact, she had received a visit from Ron Hoffman earlier in the day, and he commented that he had never seen anybody in her condition with such straight fingers!

Linda slept with the TV on, so Lisa adjusted the station and volume for her. She also made sure the Lifeline was next to her hand in the bed, although they both acknowledged that at this point, Linda hadn't the strength in her hand to activate it.

That was pretty much Linda's bedtime ritual. I left at that point, though Lisa stayed a little while longer for some incidentals with Linda.

Morning Routine

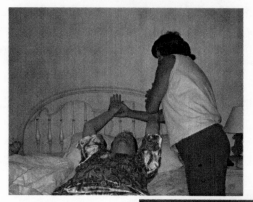

Lisa stretches Linda's
arms and legs.

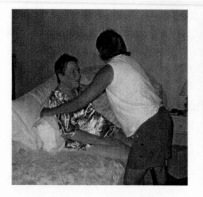

Lisa props up pillows to prepare for pivot lift transfer.

Linda is transferred to the sliding shower chair.

Linda gets a soothing hair brushing, then a scalp massage.

Lisa powers up Linda's wheelchair.

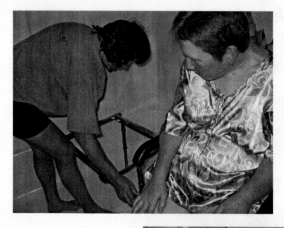

Lisa prepares to move the sliding shower chair into the tub area.

Bath time!

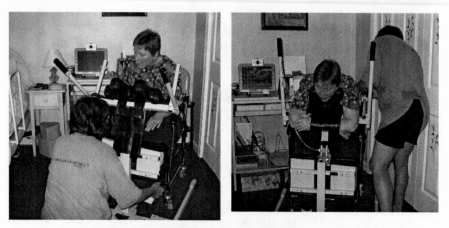

Lisa readies pivot lift for transfer to wheelchair.

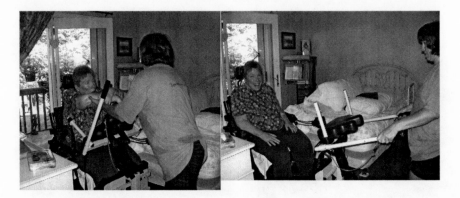

Transfer in action…..   …Transfer complete!

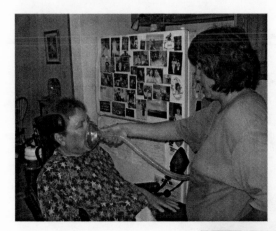

Using the cough assist
machine

Ready for morning
stroll!

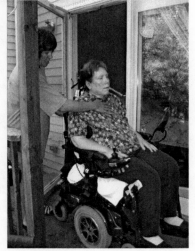

137

Bedtime Routine

Pillows have been positioned for Linda's transfer to the bed with the pivot lift.

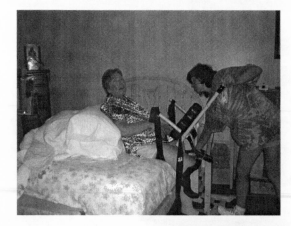

Transfer is nearly complete.

Lisa has moved Linda over and adjusts the bed.

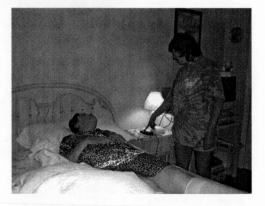

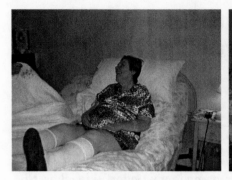

Top and bottom of bed are adjusted.   Leg and foot massage feels great!

Linda is wearing the hand contraption she and Lisa designed to prevent her fingers from curling.

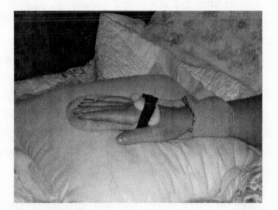

The Lifeline button is positioned close to Linda so she will have access to it if needed.

Chapter 23
More From Patty

Patty Continues Reminiscing:

I always thought Linda would have made a wonderful teacher. She was influenced by her parents to go into the business world, which I could never understand. It wasn't Linda. She was a people person. She would have been a fantastic teacher. When she was in Taiwan she did do some teaching, and she enjoyed it. When she returned home, I am sure she felt it was too late to reinvent herself, and she had to make a living, so she continued in the business world.

Linda was diagnosed with Multiple Sclerosis shortly after her marriage to Jim Burge. That was a very difficult year for her. They lived in an apartment in Rockland at the time, but later moved to a home in East Bridgewater. It was about that time that they separated for awhile.

Linda said that when the MS subsided, she and Jim went through a rough patch. Jim had been in the role of caretaker while she was sick and he had a hard time getting back to the independent Linda. Linda was always <u>very</u> independent! She liked to do things her way, and she didn't like somebody telling her, "No, you shouldn't do this because you are sick." I was extremely upset about their separation. It just hit me very hard. I didn't know anything about Jim's background at the time or what they had been through together emotionally. Linda didn't talk about Jim. She respected his privacy and I knew very little about him. I knew he was obsessive-compulsive about things and he had a little trouble at work because he was a perfectionist. My husband is like that, too. Garry and Jim related to each other because both sometimes had trouble with bosses with whom they did not agree. The separation between Linda and Jim was a real surprise. However, they did get back together after a few months, and eventually they bought a condo in Abington where they lived for many years.

Linda, Jim, Garry, and I would get together as a foursome regularly. We'd have dinner at each other's houses, play games, etc. We all got along fine. When Garry and I had our children, Linda and Jim would babysit. I remember when my sister was killed accidentally, Linda and Jim came over and volunteered to stay with the children while we went to the wake, which was very helpful. That is the kind of person Linda was. She would think about what needed to be done and what she could do to help. I never forgot that. It meant a lot to me that they would both come over and stay with our young children while we did what we needed to do.

One of the big things Linda and I would do as adults was go to concerts. We would often go to Massassoit, a small community college in Brockton, when they featured a good musical act, especially if it had to do with folk music. Either Linda or I would find something going on and the two of us would go if the guys weren't interested. We shared a love of music. As kids, we loved to listen to music together. Linda always gave me records for my birthday.

We enjoyed movies together as well. I remember we saw the first "Star Wars" movie before it became a big box office draw. We also saw "The China Syndrome" and had a detailed discussion afterwards about the implications of the movie. Linda was worried about the future of the world. There was a movie that was going to be on TV with an apocalyptic theme after a nuclear war. It got a lot of publicity and critics said it was going to be very hard to watch. Linda said she would not watch it because she felt that someday we were going to live it. She was sure that a nuclear attack or accident was inevitable in the future, and she was not interested in watching it on TV first. She rarely talked politics, but every now and then this pessimistic viewpoint about the world would surface.

Linda eventually went to a four-year college. She went to my alma mater, Stonehill. I did not realize it at the time, but Linda felt she

141

was competing with me. I had gone to Stonehill and graduated first in my class. Linda was very proud that she graduated with a 4.0 average, and was first in <u>her</u> class. So there was more rivalry there than I had realized, but we just made a joke about it. I am not sure how she knew I had been first in my class, but it must have come up somewhere along the line. Linda got her degree in business, and it took her many years because she was taking night classes. She was taking classes, constantly studying, and working full time.

Linda seemed driven to be busy, busy, busy. She did not like being alone, particularly after the divorce. In addition to her bank job, she took on a second job at Wal-Mart that was almost a full-time job. She was always working and hardly ever at home. I think she needed to keep herself occupied and busy, perhaps because of some lack in her personal life.

Linda did a lot of things with girlfriends. She had a wide circle of friends, many of whom she would get together with at Christmas time and for birthdays. She tried to draw me into her circle of friends and I was reluctant because I am not a crowd type person. Linda would not take no for an answer and she was persistent, so eventually I relented and became one of the pack. It turned out to be a good thing, and I enjoyed it.

Linda and I were great letter writers – especially when we did not see each other too much. We wrote about once or twice a month since we didn't talk as much on the phone. I was teaching, she was working and busy.

We both loved to read, so often we would share our reading selections. We enjoyed the same types of books. She turned me on to "On the Beach," which had a nuclear theme. Linda would read very sophisticated books – more so than the ordinary high school person. She was always mature for her age and tended to choose books that were more adult in nature. She definitely led me to read books that I would never have picked up otherwise. If Linda liked a book, then I usually did as well. We would lend each other tons of books. We liked romance stories with happily ever after endings. Rosamund Pilcher and Rumer Godden were two favorite authors.

Some of Rumer Godden's books were about nuns and had religious themes. Linda was Episcopalian, but was fascinated by the Catholic religion. Linda told me once that she always thought I would become a nun. I have always been a spiritual, religious person and have enjoyed the rituals and going to mass. However, I got married instead!

As an adult, I remember Linda would try to go to services whenever she could. It's not mandatory in the Episcopal Church to go every Sunday the way it is for Catholics. She said she loved receiving communion and the wine, and all the rituals. So that is another thing Linda and I had in common. We both believed in religion and God, and we were both spiritual. When we were in our twenties, we had a discussion about God. At that time Linda told me she did not believe in a heaven. She believed that when you die, the last moment you experience is your heaven or hell. I was very upset about that because I like to think that all my loved ones will be together in heaven in the afterlife. I do think that is what Linda came to believe eventually, especially after her parents died. She liked to feel that she would be reunited with them and she did believe they were watching over her. However, I was shocked and upset when she did not believe in heaven. When you are young, you want your friends to think the same way you think. I know I did.

Linda had developed early in life an interest in following the lives of celebrities. As a teen-ager she had quite a collection of photographs and autographs of TV and movie stars. She tried to entice me into this hobby, but the few photos I did send for ended up in a bottom drawer, soon forgotten and crumpled. Not Linda's: she took meticulous care of her treasures and was always eager to display and share them. This certainly reflected her penchant throughout her life for collecting and displaying a multitude of precious items. I also recall her as an adult following with avid interest the career of a musician named Jim Scott. Linda and her husband Jim had come across this talented songwriter, singer, and

143

guitarist at a local cafe. From then on, she (and her friends) took in every local performance for many years. When Jim Scott joined the Paul Winter Consort, we all went into Boston for a concert which featured sitting in the dark in a circle howling with a live wolf!

I remember a "Girls' Weekend" Linda and I enjoyed one Columbus Day, when just she and I drove up to New Hampshire. We visited Judy and John's farm, attended a concert (of course!) and we dropped in on Linda's parents who had recently moved to Milton. We talked non-stop the whole way up and back, sharing both good and bad things going on in our lives at that time. Linda was very concerned about her mother Dolly, because she was still in her housecoat when we arrived, and did not offer us any refreshments, which was very unlike her. Linda was close to both her parents, but especially to her mother, a relationship that I envied. Linda would invite Dolly along with her own friends to craft fairs and events, which seemed to me an amazing thing.

The following spring, when her mother's diagnosis of pancreatic cancer was determined, Linda stopped by our house on her way back from New Hampshire, just "because she needed to talk." This was unusual, because we always arranged our get-togethers in advance, and did not just "drop by". Linda stayed for supper and then we talked and talked.

Linda and I truly could, and did, discuss any topic or concern throughout our whole friendship. Our personalities were quite different, but I believe that we complemented each other. When we first met as teen-agers, I had no idea that our relationship would grow and nurture us for more than four decades. This was probably due mostly to Linda's sense of commitment and loyalty. She maintained several close friendships from her youth throughout her life, while for me, Linda was the only person from that same period whose friendship grew and endured.

Chapter 24
Personal Impact of ALS

Q & A with Linda, June 25, 2005

Leslie: What are some of the things you miss the most that you can't do any more?

Linda: Surprisingly, there are not too many…but there are two things that I miss greatly. One is being able to shake hands. Because of my many years in the business world, I became used to shaking hands when greeting someone. I can no longer do that and I miss it very much. Last week I interviewed a new PCA candidate, and when she walked in, she put her hand out to shake mine. I cannot extend my hand. I said to Lisa: "R. is trying to shake my hand, can you help?" And we made a joke of it. Lisa picked my hand up and put it in R.'s, and we shook. I was very impressed at the conclusion of the interview that R. remembered and when she was saying goodbye, *she* picked up my hand and shook it. A couple of weeks ago a group of friends took us to Boston to see "Menopause the Musical." There were two new people in the group, friends of other friends. When we were seated in the theater, Lisa was occupied chatting with Marcia, and one of the new people leaned across the row behind me and said, "Hi, Linda. I'm Jan. I've heard about you and I'm glad to meet you." Of course, she extended her hand, and I said to her, "I'm sorry, I can't shake." It was very, very noisy in the theater. She could not hear me, and I saw the look of discomfort cross her face. She didn't know whether I was being rude, whether I was being unfriendly, whether it was physical, she did not know. When Lisa's attention came back to me, I told her that Jan had attempted to introduce herself and tried to shake my hand, but I could not respond. Lisa got Jan's attention, and made a joke about how we were glad to meet her, and if she wants to shake hands, "Just grab her (Linda) - she can't fight you!" We laughed, and I could see that Jan understood at that point. But I often find it awkward. I personally miss it because I always liked shaking hands.

The other thing, along the same line, that I really miss is hugging and being able to initiate or return physical contact with someone. Hugs are a one way street for me now. I can receive, but I can't give back. When Lisa is with me, she will wrap my arms around the other person. When there are children, she'll put them on my lap, so I can be wrapped up in their hugs.

Now, with the new wheelchair, hugs can be hazardous because the head array is so sensitive that if my wheelchair is turned on and someone approaches to hug me, they can accidentally activate the chair and they will risk getting run over! So if Lisa is with me in a social gathering, she will completely disable the wheelchair until all the greetings have been done. We always discuss it before hand: "Be ready when you see someone coming. Shut that wheelchair down." Recently when visiting my sister there was a small party for me and several people arrived in a flurry and Lisa was not in the room, and the first person almost got run over before Lisa rushed in and powered off the chair!

When the technology involved with my equipment is NOT working, I certainly miss that. For example, when my wheelchair is on the fritz, it is a HUGE inconvenience, extremely uncomfortable, and a safety issue as well. If I ever had to vacate my condo quickly, it would be impossible if my chair was not working. That is a major concern. When the seating system is not working, I cannot alter my position, which puts stress on my whole body. In order to activate the Lifeline, positioning is critical for me. If I cannot lean the seat forward, I cannot move my hand to press the Lifeline button.

If my Mercury 2 computer will not power up, I cannot access the internet or use it for communication. So when my equipment is not working, I am at a great loss.

What this disease does to your body is horrific. Though that is the reality, I would not change it for one day because, for me at least, this disease has brought blessings that far exceed any negative aspects. It is very hard to explain, but I believe that because of this disease, I have gotten to experience deeper relationships with everyone in my life – much deeper than ever existed prior to my getting sick.

I recently said that to my sister and she actually agreed. In the past our relationship was based on fun or good times – family holidays and family vacations. Now our relationship is much deeper, not so superficial. With my friends it is unbelievable. As Pat Baylor once said, "There has not been a deserter in the group." Everyone has remained so loyal and surprisingly, even though I have become so physically limited, it does not seem to affect our good times together. We still have dinner parties, impromptu visits, we have Scrabble tournaments, we go to theater, etc. My friends are always with me when I need them to help with a chore or when it is just for a fun visit, and I feel that ALS has brought us all closer than we ever were before. One example is the way all of my friends have supported the fund raising effort for the ALS Cliff Walk. My friend Bonnie was the first to find out about it, and she suggested we form a team the following year. We did. The second year the team grew to almost 40 participants. Now it's mid-summer, and to be truthful, I was going to blow it off, but all my friends have been calling and asking if we are going again. So, I guess we are!

I have found that ALS has opened me to receiving the many, many gifts of friendship. Recently while we were away in NH, my friend Barbara came over and planted flower boxes and created a rainbow garden on my backyard deck. She did this during my absence and left a note inside the house (she has a key) that she hoped I would enjoy my rainbow garden. This is the third year Barbara has done this. Aside from the expense of purchasing all the flowers and the work involved in planting, what amazes me most is the gift of her time. It takes a lot of effort and time to do that. I cannot express my gratitude enough. I have found that people - the people in my life – are extremely generous of their time: like Leslie and the scrapbook project, and now she is recopying my entire address

147

book. But ALS has opened me up to accept those gifts, and they are far more valuable and precious than anything you can buy with money. That is why I would not change anything.

Leslie: If you had a magic wand and could turn back the clock to your pre-ALS life and wave that wand so you would not contract ALS, would you do it?

Linda: I don't believe I would. I think before I had ALS I knew how wonderful my friends were. However, I don't believe I was open to receiving all the goodness they could offer. I think I was so wrapped up in my career and my busy, busy life, and being an "in control type" personality, that I never really opened up to receive from people around me. I remember one time saying to my friend Gail that if I died tomorrow, no one would even miss me. The world would not bat an eyelash. I felt very insignificant. I don't know what I thought I should be doing. Perhaps somewhere in my mind I felt that my contribution to the world was pretty much nonexistent and non-recognized. I wasn't curing cancer. I wasn't discovering any way to save the environment. I wasn't standing the world of mortgages on its collective ear. I think I always felt in a way, invisible. However, having ALS has brought the world to my door. More and more friends bring other friends. I have gotten to know new people. I feel surrounded by people who care, and not because they feel sorry for me. I never ever get that feeling. People come, we have fun. There are many, many blessings.

Leslie: What do you think the reaction would be now if you died? Do you think the world would not bat an eyelash?

Linda: No, I no longer feel that way. I think that my friends would really miss me, which is quite gratifying.

There is another thing – which goes back to being a control freak - I always felt very insignificant in God's eyes. I felt that I was too unimportant for God to worry about my little life. ALS has taught me to put my life in God's hands. God takes care of me. Whenever I am pushed against the wall and I turn to God for help, it always arrives. So ALS taught me to let go and let God, as they say. ALS also has taught me patience and it's been a very hard teacher, but I was always doing, doing, going, going. Now I have had to learn to wait and sometimes it's very, very difficult. If I have a list in my mind of things that need to be accomplished and I am waiting for my helper to arrive, perhaps for two or three hours, I sit waiting, watching mindless TV, knowing that I want to do all of these things, but need my helper to accomplish them. It's very difficult to wait. ALS has forced me to learn patience and not go out of my mind while I am waiting. For me, that was a giant effort.

As a matter of fact, I have come to the conclusion that everything is for a reason. I can clearly recognize two reasons for my having ALS. One, because I needed to learn patience, and I believe God is teaching me that through ALS. The other reason is to be instrumental in helping Lisa to reclaim her life and career as a nurse.

Leslie: I know it was difficult, but what was it like for someone who is so fiercely independent to lose that independence in little steps? For example, when you couldn't drive anymore, or work anymore, and your independence was chipping away in bigger and bigger chunks. At any point did you just accept that this is the way it is going to be? I remember when you first had this disease and you were at my house for Passover. I was very worried about serving chicken soup with matzo balls, because I knew you couldn't cut the matzo balls, and I didn't know what to do. I didn't want you to be embarrassed. My solution was to serve the soup with the matzo balls already cut up in everyone's soup, so it wouldn't be obvious, and I would not have to say to you, "Linda, can I cut up your matzo balls?" I knew that would be upsetting to you. That's just a small example, but I am talking on a larger scale as you could not do certain things and thus had to relinquish some of your independence along the way. How did you deal with that?

Linda: Luckily my nature is such that I am able to mentally and emotionally wrap myself around the issue at hand and adjust to almost anything, given a little breathing room. As things would happen, because they were gradual, I felt that on each step of this rocky road, I was somehow able to adjust to each loss. Often I've

149

wondered if I were someone like Chris Reeve, who was out living an active life, riding a horse one minute, and the next minute, not able to move a muscle, how would I ever be able to adjust to a loss of that magnitude so instantaneously?

My situation is similar to Chris Reeve's now, but it took me over five years to get where I am. It was so gradual that while each loss bothered me, it did not devastate me. Somehow, my psyche allowed me to face and deal with each little loss. There were times it was sort of like a slap in the face because the loss would happen very suddenly. I remember at one point that I could still lift my arm and click the light switch on the kitchen wall. There was one morning I turned it off, and later in the day when I went to put the light back on, I could not do it. And I could never do it again. That was like a slap, all of a sudden, knowing that ability was gone. I could do it eight hours ago, but no more. There were other instances like that. For the most part, I was able to deal with each successive loss, problem solve around it, and find another way. Eventually, of course, there were few options left. However, even now, by the grace of God, I have been able to find ways around the obstacles, such as having the head control on the wheelchair, and my new computer.

Leslie: Do you think one of the reasons it has been difficult, but not devastating for you is because, as you have said, you have always tried to stay a step or two ahead of the disease and anticipate what was coming? Do you think that psychologically maybe you prepared yourself for an eventual loss? Could that be part of the reason it has not been so devastating for you?

Linda: I do think that. I have been lucky, I guess, because in my case, the progression has been very, very slow. Only 20% of ALS cases survive five years. I think that I am a very realistic person. From the beginning, I knew what was ahead. I set a goal to continue to live my life. I had often thought about my future retirement, hoping I would move to Vermont. Now I know that *this* is my retirement, and I made up my mind to enjoy it to the best of my ability and to live as comfortably and independently as possible. I thought ahead. I tried to look into the future far enough to put adaptations and systems in place so that when I needed them they would be ready for me. Patty Baylor refers to this stage of my life as my "ALS career." To a certain extent, I approach daily living with ALS and all of the challenges that includes, as a job. There is a lot of business involved – insurance, hiring and training people, keeping payrolls straight, dealing with red tape and health care bureaucracy, and searching for equipment. To a great extent, I have approached this as I approached working in the mortgage industry. It's really like a business. I think that approach has definitely helped keep my wits about me.

Chapter 25
Houston (Lifeline) – We Have a Problem!

Linda:

In early July (2005) on a Tuesday morning, R. accidentally locked the front door when she left. When Nancy came at about 12:45 for my lunch, she found herself locked out! Knowing I was stuck in the bedroom and still in the manual loaner chair (my power chair was out for repairs), Nancy walked around to my back deck where we could communicate through the slider (which was closed because the AC was running). I hit the Lifeline button to call for the fire department to come use their key to let Nancy in.

My TV was quite loud, and my non-power chair was faced away from the phone when the respondent came over the telephone speaker. Between my distorted speech and the background noise from the TV, he had trouble understanding me. Asked if I needed help, I answered yes. When asked what was wrong, I said "fire" to make it simple. The fire department has to come in full regalia even if they know it's just to unlock my door, so it made no sense to struggle with a long explanation. He asked again and I answered the same way. This was repeated four times and even Nancy - on the deck - heard me!

At last this guy told me he was going to get me help. Next, I was shocked to hear him in the background calling each person on my personal call list, including Nancy who was on my deck and not at home to get the call! I heard him leave messages on one machine after another. Finally after about ten minutes, he came back on my intercom to say he couldn't reach my friends, so he would call the fire department!

The Fire Department arrived in less than five minutes and let Nancy in.

That late afternoon Lisa (who had received a cell phone message from the Lifeline guy when she was on a sailboat!) called Lifeline for an explanation of the whole earlier episode. They told us their records showed that it sounded like I was saying "Fire," but their guy wasn't absolutely sure, and he couldn't hear any smoke alarms going off in my home so he decided to try to reach one of my personal contacts first.

If there was even the slightest chance of fire, shouldn't he have called the fire department first? Wouldn't it be better to err on the side of safety?

Lisa explained my speech issue and instructed them to note in the file to call the fire department if I can't respond and/or be understood over the intercom.

Thursday afternoon, two days after the lockout incident, I tested the Lifeline before Shauna went off her shift. The signal went through but the call was dropped and disconnected before Lifeline's respondent answered. They didn't respond for about 25 minutes, at which time they called my regular phone instead of speaking with me over the Lifeline intercom. Shauna explained to them that I could not answer the house phone and it was critical that the system work promptly and properly. We performed several more tests with unsatisfactory results and were ultimately advised to call the business office and make an appointment for a technician to visit my home. Shauna scheduled that for Friday when Lisa would be here with Design Able (a company that makes and repairs powered mobility equipment for the disabled), hoping she could help with both issues at one time.

Friday an aged technician named Herb came and changed the entire Lifeline phone unit but his testing showed the problem persisted. He set it up so that if I placed a call, they would dial me back on my regular phone which would ring three times and then the intercom would pick up and I would be able to communicate over the intercom. This process would take about five minutes, too long in a real emergency. He advised us to call Verizon. We set up the earliest Verizon appointment for the following Tuesday.

153

Saturday morning we tested. The call dropped and no one ever called back! Over 1½ hours later when Nancy came to get my lunch, Lifeline called on the regular phone and it failed to connect over the intercom. Nancy told them what had transpired and they told us to repeat the test. There had still been no response by the time she left an hour later!!

Three hours later, my regular phone rang and I recognized the number, but could not get to it in time to answer. Moments later the Rockland Fire Department arrived! My friend Lt. Don Hussey had been off duty and heard the call come over his home scanner, so he rushed over. I explained the situation about the unanswered test of more than three hours earlier and told him I had not pressed the signal since.

Knowing the Lifeline equipment, the firemen could see from the lights not flashing that I hadn't activated my signal device.

The RFD called Lifeline from my home and the respondent insisted that I had signaled just a few minutes ago!

The firemen performed several tests without success, and Lt. Hussey told Lifeline they had better make this a priority repair because it obviously was <u>not</u> Verizon's issue.

All was quiet until about 9:30 when Lisa was here. My regular phone rang and Lifeline was calling to see if I needed help! They told Lisa they had just received a distress call from my button. I wasn't wearing the button and Lisa told them this. They insisted we had pressed the button without realizing because the button "is very sensitive." Lisa told them the device was lying on the bureau in the other room and we were not even near it. They responded "Ms. Burge's cat probably walked on it!!!" Lisa demanded to speak with a manager. He was no help, but did let slip the fact that they had been running on a backup system all weekend and there had been some delayed response times. He also told Lisa to test again and he would call back in five minutes. We tested at 10:02, but he never called.

At 11:45 PM the phone rang. "Did I need help?" They insisted we had just signaled them and that the system was working fine. When Lisa queried about running off the backup, they knew nothing about it.

I went to bed sans signaling device because I figured it was currently useless. At 1:30AM my regular phone rang and caller ID announced Lifeline's number. Four minutes later I was entertaining RFD in my bedroom again!

The RFD could see no lights flashing on my Lifeline phone unit. They were furious, not at me, but at Lifeline. They called Lifeline, who insisted I had activated my device just a few minutes earlier. RFD told them I was in bed - ten feet away from the device which was lying on the dresser. Lifeline responded that I probably got out of bed, walked to the bureau, pressed the button, got back in bed, and forgot I had done it! I wish! When RFD explained this was impossible because I'm a paralyzed quad, they went back to the "maybe her cat or dog or bird stepped on it" approach. The RFD hung up in frustration. Then we all enjoyed a laugh over the ideas Lifeline had suggested.

The saga continued and I was very uneasy knowing I couldn't get help in bed at night. Monday morning I had Shauna contact the customer service department, and she finally demanded and got a manager named Jane H., who actually listened and admitted they had done a system upgrade over the weekend and had been running on a backup system with two and three hour delays in response time. However, since my problem seemed to have presented on Thursday, prior to the upgrade, and since the system was now supposedly working properly, there seemed to be more to my problem. Shauna strongly emphasized the helplessness of my situation with their service malfunctioning. She stressed their liability should an emergency arise leaving me unable to get help through their system, with which I have a contract. Jane was properly concerned and apologetic. She told us to test once more and not again until I heard back from her, and she promised to call back by end of day.

Jane followed through. Over the next couple of days we had many conversations and tests and another unnecessary visit by RFD. Lt. Hussey read her the riot act. Jane admitted the system upgrade was complete and now operating properly. Verizon checked lines and ruled out Verizon as the source of the problem. Finally Jane said she had one last recourse which was to consult a programmer.

Wednesday morning Jane called and told us to test. Miraculously it worked, promptly and correctly. Two subsequent tests produced perfect results. Jane followed up with a call and explained that the problem originated on the Tuesday I called when Nancy was locked out. When they programmed in Lisa's instructions to "call RFD if they couldn't hear or understand," they entered data into an incorrect field and screwed up my entire system.

Because I experienced the malfunction simultaneously with their own system upgrade issues, nobody prior to Jane gave any credence to my complaint. They just assumed my problem would go away when they were no longer running on backup!

I asked Jane why the respondents had insisted so adamantly that the system was working fine. Jane said the respondents had not been informed about the upgrade and associated delays so they couldn't "slip" and say something that might cause panic among subscribers.

Jane was genuinely apologetic and promised three months free service. I also asked for reimbursement of $110 I paid Lisa out of pocket because I exceeded my allotted payroll while dealing with the issue. I intend to pursue this compensation!

One last ridiculous thing happened this Monday at 5:30 PM, five days since Jane solved the problem. A Lifeline customer service rep called and left a message on my answering machine saying he had received a memo that I was experiencing equipment problems and to call him back if I was still having trouble. I won't return his call!

Post Script to story:

A few weeks later, Jane H., the customer service manager who had gotten to the bottom of the problem and finally resolved it, had her representative, Amanda, call me to follow up on everything. Amanda wanted to know whether I had gotten a bill from Verizon for checking the outside lines. I told her my bill came and so far, no charge from them. Amanda said if there was a charge in the future, that I should send the bill to Jane and they would take care of it. Also, they would give me three full months billing credit for the Lifeline service at $45.10 per month.

Patty Baylor, who made one of the calls to Jane, had mentioned to them that I had paid one of my PCAs $110 out of pocket because we ran over budget for my PCAs due to the Lifeline malfunction. Amanda asked me to fax her a copy of that check and they will repay that. So I am satisfied at the effort that they made to remedy the situation. I feel that Jane H. truly understands the term "customer service."

Chapter 26
Vignettes

Bathing Safety

Looking back, it's a laughable experience, but at the time, it was scary. I was still living in the townhouse condo, and normally I showered, but one afternoon I got it in my mind, "Wouldn't a long soak in the tub be nice!" Well it was almost a *lifelong* soak in the tub! I filled the tub, climbed in, I soaked, and I enjoyed it thoroughly. I got ready to get out, drained the tub, went to stand up... and could not get to my feet. There were no bars in that tub, but nothing would have helped. I could not stand. I tried to be calm and I thought, "Okay, breathe and gather your strength. You can do this."

It was summertime and the room was not cold, but I was wet and naked, and chilling rapidly. I decided to turn the water back on to warm up, then drain it out and try again. Looking back, I don't know whether the warm water contributed to the weakness. It may have. Up until that time, if I was on the floor, I could get back to my feet, so I assumed that in the tub I could get to my feet as well. I drained the tub again, and with all the power I could muster, I attempted to get to my knees at least. Nope – it was not going to happen. I could not get out of that tub. Ultimately, I ended up - with every bit of strength that I had, literally swinging myself out onto the floor. I flopped over the side of the tub. Like a beached whale, I was now wet and cold on a tile floor. Somehow, I managed to crawl on my hands and knees to the toilet and use the base to pull myself up. I remember I sat on the toilet and I first started to cry, and then I was laughing. I remember just laughing and laughing, and thinking I would be the $10,000 prizewinner on *America's Funniest Home Videos*! When I finally had the strength, I managed to walk into my bedroom, climb on the bed and pull the covers over me. I was shivering. As I slowly warmed up, the event kept replaying in my head. I felt like I was a movie director watching the scene in my mind... There I was, just sitting on the toilet while gasping for breath and laughing at the utter absurdity.

Ultimately, I recouped and got dressed. I called my friend Gail, and I said to her "I have just taken the last tub bath I will ever have." It was comical by then, but it also was like a revelation and a realization of the future. It struck me full force that my life was changing rapidly and drastically.

Another Story
One afternoon after I had become wheelchair bound, I was home at my condo and nature was calling. I needed to move my bowels. I had stomach cramps, and I was in agony. The helpers that I had coming in and out were evidently between visits. Ultimately, I lost control and messed all over myself. I called several different health aides, who, against the rules of their company, were working for me under the table, but none of them was home. Finally, in desperation, I called one who had been very helpful to me who lived in Cohasset, at least 45 minutes from here. Thankfully, she was home. I explained my predicament, and God Bless her, on her own time, not working for the agency, she drove out here from Cohasset, cleaned me up, changed me, and got me all squared away. I always felt that that was a real act of mercy and compassion. She was on her own time. She could have said, "Sorry, I can't do it," but she never hesitated. I was overwhelmed by her goodness in doing that.

A Funny Occurrence
One day before I had the tub cut out, I caught my foot on the edge of the tub trying to get out, and I fell face down and stark naked on the bathroom floor. I hit the Lifeline, and the firemen came out within five minutes. The bathroom door was closed, but not latched, so as I heard the firemen coming in, I yelled, "Stop wherever you are! I am in a <u>very</u> compromised position!" One of the young firemen came to the other side of the door and asked me if I was hurt. I said, "No, I've fallen and I can't get up, and I am lying here stark naked." He turned to his co-firemen and told them

159

to wait where they were. He asked me if I had a blanket he could use. I told him there was a blanket on the closet shelf. He was so cute. He said, "Okay, when I count three I will open the door, close my eyes, throw the blanket on you, and we will get you up." He did just that. It happened very quickly. He threw the blanket over me, covered me, rolled me, and had me on my feet. Later I told my friend Betsy the story. Betsy is married to a fireman. She laughed hysterically and commented that firemen also are very good at *un*dressing people!

Because of the dimensions of my tiny bathroom, once I started going in with my wheelchair and standing up and using a walker to maneuver in there, if I fell, the firemen had to fight their way in to get to me. Normally to get me on my feet, one fireman would end up standing in the shower, and another would be on the rug and they'd boost me up. After one such fall, one of the firemen commented that he spent more time in my shower than he did in his own!

A Somewhat Comical Fall

I was moving dishes from a cabinet in my dining room to my kitchen. These particular dishes were antique china that I had collected piece by piece over several years. One of my friends, Judy W., also collects the same pattern. I had told her that when I am gone, my dishes are hers. (I have put that in writing for my sister to be sure that my friend will get these dishes.) So I was carrying them, a few at a time, in a basket hooked over the handle of the walker. I got a few steps into the kitchen and an unexplained fall occurred. I crashed to the floor. The basket of dishes was under me. I heard "CRASH." I hit the Lifeline, and the firemen came out. When they walked in, I said to them, "Be careful when you try to move me. I am lying on top of a basket, and I believe it is full of broken antique china that I was trying to carry." I warned them that there might be broken glass. I did not want to get cut. Very gently, they pulled me off the basket and the dishes, and one of the firemen said, "You won't believe it. They are completely unscathed." They helped me to my feet, and I could not believe that those dishes had not broken - not a chip, not a crack. The firefighter commented that it was amazing. Then he said with a smile, "I guess that's how they get to be antiques. They are tough, just like you." It was funny.

A Visit from R.'s Son

Recently I hired a Haitian woman to be one of my PCAs, and I found her to be a lovely person, maybe a little scattered from time to time. She is working out and I am hoping she will be with me for awhile. One afternoon, due to car problems, she had to take a taxi here from Brockton to Rockland. I estimate it must have cost at least $35, and she only gets a $10.84 per hour wage. However, she did not want to miss her shift. She was forced by circumstances to bring her seven year old son with her. When I learned that he was coming, I had a very negative reaction because I have had a lot of frustration with people bringing small children here to work. This is not the environment for a disruptive small child, who is also a distraction to the health care worker. My home is a potential danger to the child. I waited for R. to arrive and I mentally rehearsed the speech I would give - that it was not acceptable to bring her son. This would be one time only.

They arrived, and this little boy came in with his mom and he said, "Hello, Miss Linda. I am happy to meet you." Well, I was immediately impressed and began to melt. R. introduced her son, Allain, and she asked him to tell me what they had discussed on the journey here. Allain proceeded to recite: "I have to behave. I have to be quiet. I have to respect your home." His mother said, "What else?" This little boy said, "I know Miss Linda cannot move her arms or her legs, and I know Miss Linda talks differently, but she is just like we are."

I was just so, so impressed! Interesting about the speech issue: I made it a point to talk with him, but not through his mother as an interpreter. In the beginning, of course, he was struggling with my distorted speech, and it was so cute. After three or four minutes, his face brightened up flashing a big smile, and with an incredulous expression he said, "Miss Linda, I can understand you!" I said, "I thought you could." He called to his mom and said, "Mum, I can understand!"

161

I told him that because of ALS I talk very low and very slow. Then I said, "If you listen carefully, you probably can understand, and if you don't, ask me and I will try again."

He is a credit to his mom, and I really enjoyed the visit.

Post Script:
R. said it was an emergency and she would never, ever, ever bring her child to work again. Truth be told, I wouldn't mind. He was an absolute pleasure!

E-Mail to the Rescue (almost)
Linda was nothing if not resourceful! On one particular occasion, one of her health care workers did not show up for her shift. This was a major problem for Linda. The only time she could eat or go to the bathroom was when a PCA came for her shift. To complicate matters, Linda's phone was off the hook, making any phone communication impossible. By 8 PM, Linda was in a bad way, and her last resort was to try e-mailing her friend, Leslie!

The following are the actual e-mail correspondences between us:

Sent: 9/29/05, 8 PM
Subject: Re: Please help !

Hi Leslie-

Taking a shot that you're on-line right now and sending an SOS! If you get this please call Lisa (781-351-****) and ask if she can come at 9:00 (instead of 10:00).

My phone is off the hook so I can't call. Open phone line means no Lifeline, too, so e-mail is my only hope. And you're my only friend who checks frequently.

R. never came so I need to eat and have a bathroom break. Before my phone disconnected I talked to her son and husband who didn't know where she was but said they would have her call me if she got home. Now she can't get through if she tries because my line is open!

Two hours till Lisa is scheduled so I'll be okay, but a snack and bathroom break would be nice! And I need to reach R. to confirm she'll show up tomorrow as scheduled. There's definitely something wrong!

You can put tonight's predicament down as another "bump in the road."

Please call Lisa if you get this before her scheduled 10PM shift.

Thanks, Linda

Normally, Linda was right – I would have been on my computer early in the evening tending to various projects. However, not on that night! Read on.

Sent: Thursday, September 29, 2005 9:44 PM
Subject: Re: Please help !

Hi Linda-
I feel terrible. Normally I am online by 8, but on Thursdays I watch *Survivor* and *The Apprentice*, so I don't get on until 10. However, at the half point time on *Apprentice*, since I had a lot to do, I decided to get online. Yours was the first message I checked, and I immediately called Lisa. Sorry – I wish it could have been earlier.

Linda, I don't know what you are going to do about R. You are right, something is definitely wrong. She seems so nice, but a responsible person just doesn't neglect showing up when another person is counting on them. This is a major problem, as it has happened before.

I plan on coming over next Tuesday. Let me know a good time to come.

Hope you were able to hold out until Lisa's arrival.

ttyl,
Leslie

Two days later, Linda sent the following e-mail:

Sent: Saturday, October 1, 2005, 10:20 PM
Subject: Re: Please help !

Hi Leslie-

Do I get a perfect score for being resourceful Thursday night? And do I know my old friend well? Thanks for your help. Lisa arrived in time to feed me and avert a toileting disaster. I wanted her to be out of here by 11:30 because she had to get up at 6:30 next day for school. Thanks to your help, it worked out for us both.

Tuesday will be fine for a visit, anytime after 1:30. If you plan on interviewing me, it can't be too long. I just get too fatigued trying to talk at any length.

See you Tuesday,
 Linda

Linda found out why her health care worker hadn't shown up for her shift on that Thursday, and she e-mailed Patty's sister Bonnie about the episode (with a cc to me). It is an incredible – and scary story. Linda's e-mail began with a response to a previous e-mail from Bonnie.

Sent: Saturday, October 01, 2005 9:48 PM
Subject: Re: Linda in Limbo

Dear Bonnie,

Thanks for the empathetic words. I am going to agree with you about other people being unable "to imagine what [I] go through on a daily basis." Life with ALS truly is the most challenging and difficult "job" I've ever had. In retrospect, it makes all my frustrating years in the "dog eat dog" mortgage industry look like a day at the beach! I had one tough job after another, but they were just that: jobs. At the end of the day, it was over until the next day and it was never life-threatening. The ALS experience is constant and unrelenting, 24/7, and often openly life-threatening. When I worked in mortgages I always thought of myself as a tough businesswoman. I managed to survive and keep my career alive while so many others in the industry suffered repeated layoffs. Life with ALS has proved to me just how tough and how much of a survivor I am!

When these little "disasters" happen I seldom feel panic. My problem is trying not to give in to anger and /or frustration. I don't handle negative emotions well at all. I have to remain positive in order to stay focused and be able to problem-solve. Thank God I'm usually successful, but not always.

R.'s life is an enigma still, but THIS TIME she had an excellent excuse and her story was too bizarre to be anything but true. This will knock your socks off!

About a week ago, R. answered a newspaper ad for house cleaning 40 hrs./wk in a home in Easton. She told me she was taking the job but had informed the employer that she could work no later than 4 PM because she had to be here most suppertimes. Monday after her first day there, R. told me she really didn't think she would stay at that job long because the lady was a "rich snob" (This surprised me because I've never heard R. make disparaging comments.) and had followed R. around all day while she cleaned her 11 room house, which was basically already clean to begin with. R. and I couldn't imagine any home short of a Newport mansion that could possibly require 40 hours weekly cleaning.

Next day, R. arrived here very upset. The lady had told her to follow her in her car to Milton to clean her "son's" home! R. protested that she worked for the lady and not her son. The lady said, "My dear, it's all in the family." She left R. alone in the huge unfamiliar house in Milton. Every few hours she came back to check on R. Long after 4:00 she finally showed up to dismiss R. for the day and guide her to the highway. R. advised her that she didn't wish to continue with the job and was giving the lady 2 weeks notice.

After listening, I thought, "I bet this woman is running an unlicensed, undisclosed cleaning service she staffs with immigrants and aliens under the guise of hiring them to clean in her own home. She probably gets $35+/hr. and she keeps the surplus over the $9.50/hr. she pays R. and others." I didn't say this to R., however.

Thursday (R.'s missed shift here) R. was told she was being driven in the lady's car to clean her "friend's" house in Assonnet! R. protested but the woman insisted they leave R.'s car in Easton. When they reached the Assonnet destination, it was in the middle of nowhere, a newly constructed house with no phone and toilets not yet installed. R. was left there all alone to clean up after the construction crew. The woman said she would pick R. up about 3:00. The danger of the situation didn't fully register until after the woman abandoned her! R. had no cell and was completely alone in a place where no one in the world except that woman knew where she was. R. became very angry and terrified as time passed.

The "employer " finally returned for her after 7 PM! When they got back to Easton and R. had her car, she told the woman she quit! She finally got home about 8:30 but couldn't reach me because my phone was off the hook. She was so upset she took sleeping meds and went to bed.

She called me Friday at 7:30 AM and left an emotional apology on my machine. She came at 5 PM and told me the whole tale. This has got to be illegal! R. is considering calling the Attorney General.

While R. was here Friday, D. called, blowing me off for this morning, which would have been her final shift. (I say good riddance!) R. immediately offered to come at 7:30 AM to get me up, showered and dressed today before she went to her other Saturday patient. Then she came back here at 3 PM and stayed till 7:15 PM doing housework and getting me a meal. So for now she has redeemed herself!

Bonnie, I'm sending a copy of this to my friend Leslie who also knew R. was missing. Please forward this to your sister Patty for her entertainment!

Visit when you can.
 Lucky Lindy

Physical Therapist, John Matson

From the beginning, Linda felt that her physical therapist, John Matson, was extremely important to her physical well-being. He not only gave her a purpose and a goal to strive for with her physical exercises, but John was a great emotional support as well. In June of 2001, there was a very real threat that Linda was going to lose the visits from the one professional person she thought had helped her most with her ALS. The following excerpt was part of the letter she had sent thanking me for the birthday tea party I had given her.

June 2, 2001

… Speaking of John, it looks as if I am reaching the end of the road with his help, at least for the time being. Blue Cross is dragging their feet on approving any more visits from him. In order for them to authorize his visits, he has to demonstrate that my situation is improving because of him. His helping me to maintain a given level is not enough to satisfy Blue Cross's requirements. Since my disease is progressive and going only in one direction (downhill), it is difficult to demonstrate improvement. John is doing his best to try to keep me in the VNA system, so that Blue Cross will continue to pay for my home health aides. Now he is requesting approval for an occupational therapist to come out and try to help me with some of the things that have gotten worse since their last visit, such as the fact that I can hardly write at all now, and my range of motion is making it so difficult for me to reach anything in the kitchen, prepare food, etc. If Blue Cross approves a visit or two from the occupational therapist, that will keep me in the system a little while longer and the health aides will go along for the ride with no cost to me. If not, I will be thrown into the "private pay" classification and I will have to pay out of pocket for the health aides which is about $25 per hour. I'm not going to cry poor mouth, because I can pay for this, thank God, but it would be financially advantageous to me if Blue Cross

166

kept footing the bill. I have known all along that this would happen eventually, and that from here on in this is how the game will be played, with me sometimes being covered by Blue Cross/VNA, and sometimes having to pay out of pocket. The disappointing part to me is that I will not be able to have the physical therapist outside of the Blue Cross/VNA network. The VNA does not offer physical therapy through "private pay." Of all of the professional people who have come into my life since the beginning of my illness three years ago, John Matson has been the most help to me both physically and emotionally. He has just been a tremendous support and I will miss his weekly visits. I will miss his humor, and his encouragement. And it will be very challenging for me to motivate myself to keep up with all of my exercises, when I know he is not coming in to check on me and to work with me. But I know I will keep doing them, as long as I can because they do help me maintain some semblance of mobility. And, when this routine becomes too difficult for me, it will be time to get back on the active list as John's patient so that he can help me work out a new routine as needed.

(The next chapter explores this issue.)

The following week, Linda wrote a letter to John to let him know how vital he was to her life.

June 10, 2001

Dear John:

The designer of this card must have personally been or known someone in a situation similar to mine. It is perfect! I purchased it almost two years ago when I was enrolled in Doctor Russell's clinical trial of a drug being tested on ALS patients. (The drug half killed me, but it did get me connected with the Lahey Clinic!) I have saved the card ever since, waiting for the right moment and the right recipient to whom to send it. You, Sir, are the lucky winner!

During the more than two years that medical science has been trying to assist me living with ALS, I have encountered so many physicians, medical professionals, occupational and physical therapists, social (ugh!) workers, etc., etc., etc. Of them all, **John, you have been the most help to me,** both physically and emotionally. You have created an exercise routine that works for me, sort of like being my own personal trainer! You have helped me overcome so many new physical obstacles as they arose, and have found alternative ways to manage those very same problems as they returned to confront me yet again. You have helped me deal with a couple of the emotionally dark days. You have gone the extra mile, doubling as an occupational therapist and coming up with solutions for my "technical difficulties," such as the invention of the Matson/Watson Dryer Door Handle, devising a way to make my bed bar cease migrating, helping me obtain much-needed safety equipment, silencing the screaming wheels on my walker, and not to be forgotten, bringing in my mail!

167

Your initial visit to evaluate my case took place on what has thus far been the worst day of my ALS experience! On that day I was forced to finally stop working, when I could not even ascend the one stair into the office. Brought home from work and carried into the house in my wheelchair, because I couldn't even walk after making several attempts to climb that one stair, I was drained and traumatized, and terrified of what might occur next in my life. I was clawing and clinging for control by my "emotional fingernails." The only thread remaining for me to grasp onto was that the VNA was sending out a physical therapist to evaluate my case and set up a program to help me.

And then this "kid" with a clipboard (John Matson) arrived at my door, dashing the last of my weak hopes! How could someone so young possibly have enough maturity and experience to be able to understand my situation and get me the help I desperately needed?!! I cannot recall how I presented myself to you on that opening interview. Rude? Uncooperative? Possibly! I do remember feeling completely exhausted and just wanting you to leave me alone so I could rest. I was certain you and I were both wasting our time, and I just wanted you to take your clipboard and your questionnaire and go away!

How wrong was I? Completely wrong! From that day forward, your levels of maturity and professionalism have astounded me. You know how to meet your patient on the patient's level, and how to work with the patient where she/he is coming from. For such a young man, you are amazingly experienced, with a good deal of business acumen. You have perception, patience, compassion, and a wonderful sense of humor. (And we all know that laughter is the best medicine.) You also can exhibit enough authority to get cooperation from a patient with a very stubborn nature! You have a rare and special talent for what you do. In your line of work, it would be easy to get burned out. Please do not ever allow that to happen. If it starts to get to be too much for you at some point in the future, you could always take a sabbatical and lay a few bricks for a while, right?!

On my darkest day last December, John, you took a stronghold on me that began the process of pulling me back from the precipice. Using your professional skills, patience, encouragement, support, and humor, you enabled me to forget for a time the incontrovertible fact that, before this disease has finished killing me, it will have turned me into a pathetic freak by stealing my personal dignity and my ability to control my life. During these past few months **you have been a bright spot in my life, making me feel like a real person.** If it would in any way help your career, or your paycheck, I would be very happy to write a brief letter commending you to your supervisor (everybody has a boss!). Having been in business all my adult life, I am aware how the most well-intentioned words sometimes have a way of being turned against people, so I would gladly send a copy of my letter to you prior to sending it to your supervisor. That way you could review it to be certain that I wasn't saying anything that could backfire! If you would like me to do this, please give me your supervisor's name and address, and the address where I can mail a copy to you for review.

Thank you for <u>everything</u> you have done for me.

168

With sincere appreciation,
Linda

PS - Enjoy an iced coffee on a hot summer day, and remember the positive difference that you made in this patient's life.

Chapter 27
Battles with Vendors

Self Advocacy

On numerous occasions, Linda expressed to me the importance of self advocacy to preserve and protect herself through this disease. She had no spouse or other such person to be her "mouthpiece" when necessary. The reality was that because Linda was so intelligent and articulate, *she* was the best advocate she could have had. Linda was no shrinking violet, and if she felt that an injustice had been done to her, she was going to set it right. She had the will and determination to do whatever she had to do to get things back on track. ALS may have wreaked havoc on her body, but it left her brain intact.

There are plenty of able-bodied people who simply do not have the ability to express themselves with the clarity, lucidity, and agility of language that Linda had. She could get right to the point and hit the nail on the head every time.

In June of 2001, Linda was abruptly told that her insurance was terminating the services of her physical therapist. How could this be? Her physical therapist was like her lifeline. She knew physical therapy was not going to improve her condition, but it gave her a focus and helped her cope with each successive loss of function. Despite the fact she was in shock at this sudden disclosure, she took immediate action.

By the next day, Linda had composed and sent off two letters that were thoughtful, to the point, and extraordinarily powerful. The letters went to the Senior Vice president and Chief Medical Officer of Blue Cross Blue Shield, and Linda's case manager at Blue Cross Blue Shield. Rather than explain what she wrote, I have reproduced the letters here.

Certified Mail/Return Receipt Requested

June 22, 2001

Blue Cross Blue Shield of Massachusetts
25 Newport Avenue Extension
Mail Stop 12-21
North Quincy, MA 02171

Attention: Christine Churchill

Dear Ms. Churchill:

Thank you for your message on my machine this afternoon, though it was unnecessary for you to call me. Trying to obtain proper mailing addresses for you and James Fanale, M.D., V.P./Chief Medical Officer, I dialed the toll free number. Reaching just an automated answering service, I next dialed your extension, but got your voice mail. Thinking any "live" person could provide the needed addresses to me, I did not leave a message on your machine. Rather, I proceeded to dial random 5 digit sequences, connecting with four voice mails, one after another. On my fifth attempt a real representative (in your psychiatric department!) actually answered her phone! I apologized for bothering her, and asked her for the mailing addresses I required. She provided your address but said she would have to make a phone call to determine Dr. Fanale's correct address and would call me back. (I had the curious feeling she had to call someone for permission before providing me with his address.) She asked me if I wished to leave a message for you, but I told her I did not. This representative did call me back in just a few minutes, courteously leaving Dr. Fanale's address on my own machine. (Due to my mobility impairment, I let all incoming calls go to my machine.) Obviously, your co-worker told you that I had called, because minutes later you also left your message that you hoped she had given me what I needed.

Since I came under "case management", you have, within the confines of your job description, been very helpful to me and I want to thank you for that. Your job is a difficult one in which you must attempt to satisfy and assist the patient at the least possible expense to Blue Cross. Your first loyalty must be to the employer who, after all, signs your paycheck! To me, you have always been accessible, courteous, empathetic to my plight as a 54-year-old victim of ALS, and knowledgeable about this horrific disease. When I desperately needed a bath transfer bench, Blue Cross would not authorize funds to purchase this equipment. At that time, you even went so far as to put me in touch with a person outside of your company who had an almost new bench to give away. I truly appreciate the "extra mile" you went to help me obtain that vital safety equipment.

Considering my history with you, the events of this past week dealt me quite a blow, leaving me feeling betrayed and disappointed!

171

Monday, 6/18/2001, you called expressing concern over two recent falls I had. During our conversation, you suggested that I should no longer be living here alone. I told you that the only other option for me is a nursing home and I absolutely am not yet at the point where I require that type of care. We discussed the fact that I would still have falling accidents even if I lived with a dozen family members, or in a nursing home. I told you that I wear the "Lifeline" necklace, and live less than five minutes away from the fire department/emergency medical services. I reiterated the experience of a family member of mine, who fell in a nursing home and lay on the floor for almost an hour before she was discovered. You acknowledged that, unfortunately, these things are known to happen in nursing homes. We also discussed the fact, and you agreed, that a nursing home environment would in and of itself limit my mobility, likely contributing to my more severe and rapid disability, ahead of the actual progression of my disease. You said that ALS is a progressive disease, a fact of which I am completely aware and need no reminder! I assured you that, although I reside alone, people from my wide and faithful circle of friends visit on a nearly daily basis, bringing me home-cooked meals, and helping me with various little household chores.

You said that knowing this you felt better, and that you were just concerned that the help Blue Cross provided for me was what I needed. I reaffirmed to you that the home health aides who help me shower and dress, and the VNA's physical therapist are invaluable to me. I cited some specifics about recent help the physical therapist has given me, in such critical areas as being able to move around a little bit in my bed. I thanked you for your help and our telephone call was concluded.

The ax was dropped on Thursday, 6/21/01. My physical therapist, John Matson, arrived with "discharge" papers for me to sign, because Blue Cross had refused to authorize his request for continuation of his visits! I felt as if I have been struck by an automobile! After all, I had spoken with Christine Churchill only three days earlier, talking about how important visits from the physical therapist are to my maintaining mobility and being able to maintain my independent living status a while longer. Had you known all along that this vital benefit was being taken away from me? All the while that you were expressing concern for me during our phone conversation, had you really been privy to this critical information and "lied" to me by its omission from our conversation?

Giving you the benefit of every doubt, perhaps you did not know about this change when we had talked on Monday. But by today, Friday, 6/22/01, when you left a message for me regarding my request for mailing addresses, I would expect you to have known by now about this curtailment of authorization for continued physical therapy. You made no indication of it in your phone message. Perhaps it is against Blue Cross policy for you to advise a patient when Blue Cross ceases its authorization of a particular service. Or maybe it is just not in your job description to do so. But since Blue Cross continues to expend funds to mail its claimants (me) written confirmation of each and every approved request for services, and since Blue Cross representatives (you) periodically contact claimants (me) by telephone regarding needs, it seems to me that you

172

should have recognized the severely negative impact this change in my authorized services would have upon me and that you should also be in the position to make me aware of it before the physical therapist showed up at my door with the news on Thursday 6/21/01.

Before ALS has finished killing me, it will have succeeded in turning me into a pathetic freak by stealing my personal dignity and my ability to control my life. But ALS has not yet succeeded in doing that, thanks in greatest part to the help given me by physical therapist John Matson. He helped me overcome countless new physical obstacles as they arose, and then found alternative ways to manage those very same problems as they returned to confront me yet again. Using his professional skills, patience, encouragement, support, and even humor, he has helped me deal with a couple of emotionally dark days that I experienced after falling incidents. He has come up with solutions for my "technical difficulties", such as designing a handle that would enable me to open my dryer door when I could no longer grip the machine's original handle, devising a way to make my bed transfer handle bar cease migrating between the mattress and box spring, helping me obtain much needed safety equipment, and silencing the screeching wheels on my walker. He has created an exercise routine that works for me, a routine needing constant revision, due to the progressive nature of ALS.

During the more than two years that medical science has been trying to assist me living with ALS, I have encountered so many physicians, medical professionals, social workers, occupational and physical therapists. Of them all, **John Matson has been without a doubt, the most help to me, and his visits have made the biggest difference in my life. And now Blue Cross has refused to authorize continuation of physical therapy services for me!**

Ms. Churchill, I appreciate the authorized help you have been able to obtain for me thus far. Since my disease is terminal, you most likely will continue to be my Blue Cross representative for the remainder of my life, meaning that my daily health needs will continue to be in your hands. When you come right down to it, **my life is in your hands!** This letter is not in any way meant to offend or alienate you. But it is crucial to me that you and your company understand what eliminating authorization of my physical therapist means to my quality of life. **Please reconsider this decision and reinstate my physical therapist.** It is also very important to me that you understand the feeling of betrayal and loss I am experiencing due to this week's sequence of events.

I would appreciate your written response to this communication to retain for my own records. Please mail your reply to me at 45 Hobart Lane, Rockland Massachusetts, 02370.

Very truly yours,
Linda E. Burge

cc: James Fanale, M. D., Senior VP/Chief Medical Officer, Blue Cross Blue Shield of Massachusetts
cc: Attorney Richard Barry, Quincy, Massachusetts

Certified Mail/Return Receipt Requested
June 22, 2001

James Fanale, M.D.
Senior Vice President /Chief Medical Officer
Blue Cross Blue Shield of Massachusetts
Landmark Center
401 Park Drive
Boston, Massachusetts 02215-3326

Dear Dr. Fanale:

Attached is a copy of the letter that I have this day written to your employee and my case manager, Christine Churchill. I fully recognize how busy you must be in your capacity at Blue Cross. Although my letter to Ms. Churchill is lengthy, please give me the courtesy of reading it in its entirety, rather than merely scanning the copy. Reading it, I believe, will afford you a very clear picture of the details of my difficult position.

Terminally ill with ALS at age 54, I daily focus all of my energies into my battle to preserve some quality of life and personal dignity through independent living, for as long as I possibly can. There has been a great deal of business to accomplish, associated with this process of preparing to die: health care proxies and medical orders to be put on record, last will and testament to be drawn up, funeral and cemetery to be prepaid, etc. All of these things I have personally and independently accomplished with a tremendous expenditure of physical and emotional energy. **Now I find myself in the position of spending more priceless time and energy petitioning my health insurance company for reinstatement of a desperately needed home health care service.**

Thus far, weekly one hour visits by Partners Home Care, Inc.'s physical therapist have made the most significant contribution to maintaining my physical and emotional health while I still possess adequate strength and enough control of my faculties to live independently at home, with assistance. Working one hour weekly in my home with the physical therapist will not cure my Lou Gehrig's Disease. Nor will it "rehabilitate" me in the conventional sense of the word. However, **working one hour weekly with the physical therapist does enable me to remain independent by preserving some mobility and learning to work around new obstacles that develop as a result of each incremental loss associated with the relentless progression of my disease. My need for a physical therapist is ongoing and continuing. Working with the physical therapist keeps me in "the race"!**

This week, Blue Cross Blue Shield of Massachusetts denied authorization to Partners Home Care, Inc. for continued physical therapy service in my home.

174

Termination of this service will have a profoundly negative impact on my physical and mental health and my entire quality of life!

I understand that in your senior management position you are charged with fiscal responsibility to your employer, as well as an obligation to uphold company "policy". However, inherent in your profession as a physician and position with Blue Cross Blue Shield as Chief Medical Officer, do you not also have a social, even moral obligation to authorize specialized assistance to an insured person like myself, whose needs are "outside the box?" I urge you, please reconsider your decision and authorize continuation of visits to my home by Partners Home Care, Inc.'s physical therapist.

The favor of your written response to this communication is requested. I will retain your letter for my records. You may write to me at 45 Hobart Lane, Rockland, Massachusetts 02370. Thank you for your time and consideration.

Very truly yours,
Linda E. Burge

P.S. Isn't voice recognition software for the personal computer a miraculous technology?!

Enclosure
CC: Attorney Richard Barry, Quincy, Massachusetts

Though I do not have a copy of either response, I can tell you that within a week, Linda's physical therapist was reinstated and resumed providing her with services every week. Those services continued for the rest of Linda's life.

Linda was, indeed, an excellent self advocate.

~~~~~~~~~~~~~~~~~~~~~~~~~~

Another very different example shows how Linda dealt with a vendor who was being less than honest and did not seem to care very much about pleasing the customer.

Linda tells this story:

Wheelchair Woes
July, 2005

I suppose it was inevitable. My retrofitted, luxury model, souped up wheelchair was on the fritz after only two months!

The Medicare claim notice for the repair just arrived in today's mail: almost $5000! I now estimate the value of the chair at more than $31,000!!

The chair broke down July 2nd. We got someone here on July 6. It took an additional week for them to come back with a manual loaner and take my chair to the shop. The manual chair was too wide to fit through my bedroom door and tore up my woodwork. Since I couldn't move the chair myself, I became a captive in the bedroom, even eating meals and entertaining friends there. I also spent long hours lying on the bed because the chair became very uncomfortable after about one hour.

Finally last Friday (July 22, I believe), their man Tom delivered my chair. Almost immediately I could see that one of the leg rests didn't fit and was completely incompatible with my chair. They had sent him out with a component belonging to some other chair!

I immediately told Tom to call the shop to ascertain the location of my leg rest because I feared it would be delivered to someone else. He kept fussing with the wrong part, trying to force it to fit until Lisa came out of the bedroom (where she had been dealing with the Lifeline technician) and she insisted he call the shop because using this wrong component would ultimately break the power leg lift mechanism. She also made reference to a top executive with whom she had made contact earlier during this situation and who had actually offered her a job! At that point Tom went out to call the shop on his cell. He came back inside and told us the shop did have my part but couldn't say when they would deliver it to me and it definitely would not be before the next week! He told us we would need to call the shop and see when Paul could set up a future delivery date. **WRONG !!!**

When the Lifeline technician in the bedroom called Lisa, I told Tom to check out the news article about me/us hanging on the refrigerator. He was duly impressed but got nervous when I expressed intent to contact the reporter. I then shouted out for Lisa to please come and call the executive at Design Able (the company handling the repairs for my chair) without further delay. Tom rushed outside with his cell. Lisa initiated our call and was waiting to be connected when Tom rushed back in and asked her to disconnect because she didn't need to bother that executive. His face was scarlet and his tone angry as he informed us his boss was canceling the remainder of his day so he could retrieve my part from West Bridgewater, and he added (sarcastically) that this would make several other people who were waiting for him very unhappy, which I should understand. By the way, it was only about 12:40 at that time. I calmly told him that was not my problem and he left for the shop.

Slightly before 2:00 PM Tom returned with my component. He was much more relaxed and we figured he may have stopped for a beer!

We parted civilly enough.

Here's my thought: why didn't the shop send some other person to deliver the part instead of rearranging Tom's schedule, or call a courier service, or even a taxi? Surely they could have delivered the component in a more efficient way than having Tom backtrack. Also, since he finally finished here at 2:30, did they really feel it necessary to cancel his other scheduled calls – or was the error really his to begin with? We'll never know.

What we do know is that I used the ammunition I had and won another battle! But I should never have needed to resort to threats to get the situation resolved. What about sick and disabled people who haven't had their picture in the paper and who haven't accidentally made the contact of a top executive (because a previous deliveryman slipped out the name and we were smart enough to write it down for future reference)? The whole thing is just not right.

It's great to have my chair back but there are still some of the original issues regarding speeding up of its own volition. I'm pretty much convinced this is a problem inherent in the system. I just hope the chair doesn't burn out again in my lifetime.

Today a Medicare claim notice arrived showing Medicare ended up paying Design Able $7200 for the chair repair!

The notice also stated the claim for my computer: over $10,200!

It is VERY expensive to be disabled.

Chapter 28
A Night to Remember

In late October of 2005, Patty's sister, Bonnie, set the wheels in motion for a very special event in Linda's life. Curt Schilling, a pitcher for the Boston Red Sox, has been a very active fund raiser for ALS for many years. He makes personal appearances and donates a lot of his time and energies toward this cause. Knowing this, Bonnie made contact with the MA chapter of the ALS Association to see if there were any way she could arrange for a meeting with Curt and Linda. As a result of Bonnie's inquiry, an invitation was extended to Linda and her caregiver to meet with Curt at his next big fundraiser in Boston at the end of October.

The following is an e-mail that Linda received informing her of the event. This e-mail arrived only five days before the event, but it was the first Linda had heard of it. (She knew nothing of Bonnie's behind the scenes planning.)

From: Mike Travis
To: leburge@verizon.net
Sent: Monday, October 24, 2005 5:03 PM
Subject: Curt's Post-Season Reception

Hi Linda,

I spoke with Bonnie today and wanted to personally invite you to Curt Schilling's Post-Season Reception. I have put both you and Lisa Constantino on the VIP list for the event which entitles you to the VIP reception with Curt (So bring a baseball, photo, etc. and hopefully you'll be able to get his autograph.) Curt loves to meet patients and I'm sure he will be able to sign something. I hope you are able to attend, and I look forward to meeting you! P.S. I have attached all the details regarding the reception in this e-mail and if you have any questions feel free to call.

Best,
Mike

Mike Travis
Information Service and Fundraising
75 McNeil Way, Suite 310
Dedham, MA 02026
Off: (781) 326-8884 X21
Fax: (781) 326-4940
Toll Free: 1-888- CURE – ALS

Dear Curt's Pitch Reception Guest:

The Curt's Pitch for ALS 2005 Post-Season Reception has now been set for **Saturday, October 29, 2005**. The reception will be held from 6:00 p.m. to 8:00 p.m. at the State Room, 60 State Street, 33rd floor, Boston, MA, 02109. This beautiful facility is located near Quincy Market and the Old State House. The State Street building has parking available which, we have been told, is reasonable on a Saturday evening. However, there is also off-street parking in the area.

In addition to serving hors d'oeuvres, we will have a question and answer session as well as a silent and live auction. Dress is business casual to casual.

You may purchase up to two additional guest tickets at $100 per ticket at the time of making your reservation. For additional tickets, we will need the name(s), address, phone and e-mail of your guest(s) no later than October 25, 2005.

It will be **extremely important for you to RSVP as soon as you get this letter.** The cut-off for RSVP is October 25, 2005. Please RSVP with your name (and any guests), day and evening phone number, address and e-mail address to Mike.Travis@als-ma.org or call him at 781-326-8884, ext. 21. We will have representatives in the lobby of the building to escort you to the reception, so please be sure your name is on our list. We look forward to seeing you!

This sounded absolutely fantastic… except that Lisa was not scheduled to work for Linda on the day of the event, and in fact, she had made other plans for that day and evening. Obviously Linda thought she would not be able to go without Lisa, so she asked Bonnie to cancel the reservation.

As Linda remembered:

I was very disappointed, and Patty told me that Bonnie called her and she had been crying. She was crushed that it was not going to

180

work out for me to go. On Friday, the day before the event, Gregg was here for his usual Friday visit. Out of the blue, I broached the topic and he jumped right on it. He said his wife was in NY on business, and he could go with me. "Let's call and see if they can get you back on the list." He did, and they put us back on the list!

Now the problem was getting transportation. He called Ron at Compassionate Care, and while we waited as Ron checked the status of the van, Gregg then said, "You know what? I don't want to drive to Falmouth and pick up a van. I don't want to drive. I want to be a passenger." It turned out the van was not available anyway. Gregg said, "Let's call Bill's Taxi," but I told him I could not afford it. When Gregg said that he would pay for it, I said, "Call Bill's Taxi!" So we booked the taxi service for the night at a cost of about $300. (We got to the pre-reception at 5:45 and it went until 8:00. We got home about 8:45.)

Linda was back in business and very excited about attending the benefit and meeting Curt. The evening before the big event, she sent me the following e-mail:

From: Linda Burge
To: Leslie Shapiro
Sent: Friday, October 28, 2005 8:51 PM
Subject: Curt's Post-Season Reception Information

Hi Leslie -

Looks like tomorrow evening will be another chapter for the book! Thanks to Bonnie, I will be a VIP guest and hope to personally meet Curt Schilling! I invited Gregg to accompany me and he generously offered to pay for a van transport. I don't know who is more excited!

Love, Linda

From: Rick Arrowhead, President/CEO
To: leburge@verizon.net
Sent: Friday, October 28, 2005 11:46 AM
Subject: Curt's Pitch Post Season Reception Information

Dear Linda,

We look forward to seeing you at the Curt's Pitch for ALS Post Season Reception. Here are answers to some frequently asked questions that may help you prepare for the evening.

- **ARRIVAL**: Please arrive by 6:00 PM
- **ATTIRE**: Dress in Business Casual
- **OUTSTANDING BALANCES**: If you owe anything for guest tickets please bring a check, with "Curt's Pitch Reception" written in the memo section
- **AUCTIONS**: There will be a silent and a live auction
- **FOOD**: Buffet will be served
- **PARKING**: The State Room is located on the 33rd floor of 60 State Street in Boston. There are parking garages available at 60 State Street and 75 State Street; however, we do suggest you take public transportation.
- **TRAINS**: You can get to the State Room by taking the Green, Blue, Orange, or Red lines. If you take the Green or Blue lines, you'll want to get off at the Government Center stop. If you take the Orange line, you'll want to get off at the State Street stop. If you take the Red line, you'll want to get off at the Downtown Crossing stop.
- If you have any additional questions, please e-mail scott.edelstein@als-ma.org.

See you this weekend.
Sincerely,
Rick J. Arrowood President/CEO

The excitement that pervaded Linda's e-mail was quickly turned to frustration when one of her PCAs had to cancel for the morning of the big day. Linda explained in a subsequent e-mail the next day:

From: Linda Burge
To: Leslie Shapiro
Sent: Saturday, October 29, 2005 10:28 AM
Subject: Curt's Post-Season Reception Information

Hi Leslie -
 Nothing in my life is ever simple. Last night at 7 PM Heather called in sick for this morning's shift! She is very devoted and has never missed a shift in over a year of working for me and she felt very bad about canceling. Unfortunately nobody else was available to cover. Today of all days!

What I arranged was for Marybeth to be here at 7 AM to get me out of bed and toileted. She fed me yogurt and pills and seated me in my wheelchair before she had to leave at 8AM to work all day at the hospital. Now I am sitting in my nightgown waiting for R. to come after her Whitman job. She said she'll be here by 2PM, but you know R. I sure hope she makes it, because she'll shower and dress me for tonight's event. This is usually a 2+ hour job and R. moves slowly. It will be tight and no time for a snack so the yogurt will have to hold me until the reception. I hope they will serve something Gregg can manage to feed me!

Gregg will be here at 4:15 and R. will give him a crash course on my wheelchair operation. With the head control, taking me down the ramp and on and off the van requires assistance. Also he needs to learn how to disengage the motor and put the chair in manual in case of a malfunction.

Then we'll get me outside for a 5 PM van pickup. The head control makes this a challenge and it takes a few minutes, so time will be tight, indeed.

The whole operation would be much easier and less stressful if Lisa (or even Shauna) was here. Shauna is at her boyfriend's in Melrose until tomorrow. Lisa worked here till 2:00 on Wednesday and is off until Monday AM. Tonight she and Elaine will be at a Halloween party.

Bonnie began trying to put this evening together for me over a month ago. Unfortunately she never gave me any kind of "heads up." I guess she wanted to surprise me and didn't want me to be disappointed if it failed to materialize. She just assumed Lisa would be available and we could use Ron's van. When it all finally came together on Tuesday, Bonnie was devastated to learn Lisa wouldn't be available, and neither was the van. She offered to rent transport but I couldn't allow that (about $300) and I still needed a capable companion. Being Halloween weekend, all my helpers had their own plans. Lisa tried to encourage Bonnie to go with me but she didn't feel confident, so she cancelled the reservation.

I was very disappointed knowing that if Bonnie had just given us advance warning that something might be in the works, Lisa would have kept the date open and borrowed the van or at least reserved it. Bonnie was very disappointed and frustrated with herself because she had not foreseen transport and Lisa's availability as possible stumbling blocks.

Lisa is such an important part of my life that people have developed the mistaken impression that she is with me far more often than she actually is. Lisa has a very busy life that includes her other patient, school, Chelse, helping Noel, her relationship with Elaine, and a wide circle of extended family and friends. On average she is with me only about 25 hours (more or less) each week, spread out to include various shifts. Bonnie, like many others, imagined Lisa would automatically be available tonight. Lisa also was disappointed and would love to have gone. Had she known in advance, she wouldn't have made other commitments.

Anyway, yesterday when Gregg visited, I told him about it and asked him if he would have accompanied me if I had thought of him before Bonnie cancelled. He got very excited and decided to call and see if it wasn't too late to get me (and him) back on the VIP guest list. It was done! Then he called Bill's Taxi and rented their transport at his expense. I never could have afforded to go. Van transport is outrageously expensive and contributes significantly to homebound status of disabled people.

Now I don't know who is more excited, me or Gregg! And when I told John Matson about it, John was green with envy!

Leslie, you might want to rewrite this story for your book. I believe it makes clear some of the challenges ALS presents that other people never think about. For a "normal" able-bodied person, once arrangements for an event are secured, the hard part is done. That person just showers and dresses, walks out their door, perhaps all alone, gets in their car (or on the bus, train, etc.), and attends the event. When the event is over, they come home. I even have had to arrange for Marybeth to be waiting here in my house tonight to help Gregg get me back inside and then take over because by then I'll certainly need a bathroom break. For the disabled, even a pleasant excursion is quite a production. I don't know if you agree, but I think this anecdote is "book worthy."

More will follow later this week with details of the evening. I'm bringing my "Curt's Pitch for ALS" t-shirt in hopes of getting an autograph. Gregg is bringing a baseball.

Love, Linda

Let's just say that all's well that ends well! On the big day, Cinderella was ready when her coach arrived, but I will let Linda relate the events:

Saturday, October 29, 2005

When I met Curt Schilling, I was very impressed by the fact that he not only champions the ALS cause, but he goes out of his way to get involved with the patients. It was obvious because he had no difficulty whatsoever communicating with anyone of us (ALS patients). There were seven people, including me, in wheelchairs. Several of them were as verbally impaired as I am or more so. Curt had no difficulty chatting with us and understanding us. For those of us with this speech impairment, his ease with us made it very pleasurable, and to me, it indicates that he spends a lot of time speaking with ALS patients.

As for how he initially got involved with ALS – I heard that he had a friend who died of ALS. Thus, for the past 12 years, he has been committed to raising money – mostly for ALS research. I don't know how much he's raised, but it is millions of dollars.

The other six patients and I had not realized that prior to the main event, we would have a private meeting with Curt and enjoy the opportunity to speak personally with him. His easy and relaxed manner of communicating was really a treat. When your ability to speak is compromised, it makes you reluctant to chat with people who don't know you very well. With Curt, it was so comfortable.

Our private gathering lasted about 45 minutes. The other patients were in wheelchairs, like me. There was ample time for Curt to visit with everyone, and he made sure that he did. When he came over to meet me, he took my hand and picked it up. That was a gesture I truly appreciated. It indicated Curt's experience and ease with ALS patients. I had a name badge on and he said, "Hi, Linda. I am happy to meet you. Thank you for coming out on such a bad night." He was very personable. Gregg was in awe!

I did not have anything planned in my head to say to him because I had not anticipated the opportunity. I thought we might be able to get an autograph, but I did not expect a private visit. After he took my hand and said hello, it just came to me what to say to him. I asked him how the evacuees from Katrina (whom he helped come here to MA) were doing. I expected a brief, "Fine, thanks," for an answer. However, his face lit up and he started going on and on about how they were doing. He mentioned that recently his family and theirs had gotten together and there were 11 kids between the two families. He was just like any other dad relating an anecdote about the kids and the family. I found him very warm, very personable, and amazingly at ease.

There was a woman who was sitting beside me in her wheelchair. With her were her husband and two young children. When Curt approached them, the little girl asked if she could see his World Series ring. He said, "Of course!" He took it off and let her wear it while he chatted with her mom. The child was thrilled, but the parents were *really* elated.

No one asked for autographs. He made you feel like his personal guest and you forgot his celebrity. Asking for an autograph just would have been tacky.

My opinion of Curt is favorable indeed. I couldn't have felt more comfortable or been any more impressed.

Shonda Schilling (Curt's wife) was in the reception room as well, but Curt is the one who spent his time talking with us patients. It was very exciting!

In the private conference there were seven of us and our caregivers or family members, so at most there might have been 40 people in the room. If there was any security, it was invisible in this room. When we moved to the main event, Curt and Shonda were escorted by armed, uniformed police when they came out to be introduced onstage, which I found so sad. They were flanked on either side with one in front. When they were on the stage, the police positioned themselves the same way.

At the main event, there was a question and answer forum that speech-disabled people like myself could never have handled. Someone asked if his son's team won the soccer game that day. Curt and Shonda both started laughing. Curt said the team hadn't won that day because his son had managed to score a goal for the opposition! Obviously, the person who asked knew this, but it provided a lot of laughter in the room.

Most of the forum questions addressed his personal life. He said they intended to go to Arizona in a few days until the season was ready to start again. He was asked what he does in his time off and he said all he wants to do is spend time with his kids. During the baseball season, he is never home. Even when he is home, he is not home, so he wanted to enjoy his family.

At the reception, there were lots of hors d'oeuvres, wine, music, very nice entertainment, and then the formal program – awards, a silent auction, a live auction, and the dinner. There was a pasta bar, too, but all I had to eat was shrimp. For me eating is a challenge unless I am with someone who is very familiar with feeding me. So Gregg and I just had shrimp. Gregg fed me the shrimp and helped me drink Chardonnay with a straw! We joked that I was driving (my wheelchair) under the influence! I had eaten a good lunch, so I wasn't hungry. There was a huge cake for dessert, but we didn't have any of that either.

My doctor was there! When we were in the private room, the door was open. We had maybe ten minutes in there before Curt and Shonda arrived. Dr. Russell was in the doorway talking to someone. He turned around, saw me, and came running over, dragging his wife. His wife was lovely. He said to her, "This is the woman I mentioned." I said, "Watch out! You are treading on confidentiality!" He wanted to know where Lisa was. Lisa and I had just seen him that Monday. I introduced Gregg. He was chatting and chatting with me. His wife was very personable. When he saw someone else he knew come in, he excused himself, but his wife stayed. I told her that when I had seen Dr. Russell on Monday, I teased him because he had a student with him and he told the student that now my visits with him were mainly social. I said, "That's not MY fault. I have been coming here for five years to see you and I *still* have ALS!" He laughed. His wife laughed when I told her the story, but then she got very serious. She said, "You know, the older he gets and the longer he works in this specialty, that fact becomes more difficult for him to bear. He really gets frustrated."

At the main event I had parked my wheelchair quite close to the stage because there was a wonderful view out the window. We were on the 33rd floor looking right out and down on the Custom House clock tower, overlooking the harbor and it was beautiful. Gregg had gone off to get me some shrimp. The formal program began and Rick Atwood who is the ALS CEO of the MA chapter, was first up on the stage making a plea for support of the Lahey Clinic and Dr. Russell. He was going on about how their program helps manage ALS and improve quality of life for those of us with ALS. I guess I was unconsciously nodding in agreement. All of a sudden, Rick stopped, pointed to me, and said, "You can all see Linda down here in front agreeing with everything I have been telling you. If you want any details, go talk to her. Then make a generous donation!" It was funny – everyone laughed. Later in the evening, a couple actually did approach me. The woman was in a wheelchair and they told me that she is currently a patient at Spaulding Rehab and they wanted to know my opinion as to whether it would be advantageous to switch to Lahey. I explained that the Lahey's ALS clinic is "one stop shopping." In other words, any patient who goes for an appointment can see Dr. Russell, the physical therapist, a speech therapist, a social worker – whomever you might need is available on one visit. You don't have to go to multiple locations. You don't have to go running around again and again. Having one stop that covers all your possible needs is invaluable. I also told her that I have had wonderful assistance from Spaulding regarding equipment and communication. I told her that my personal advice would be to establish a relationship with Lahey and retain the relationship with Spaulding, then she will have the best of all worlds.

There was a silent auction table and a live auction for artwork. One of the pieces was a large oil painting of Curt pitching at the World Series. The artist was at the event. Bidding was a little slow. I felt embarrassed for the artist who must have been feeling somewhat unappreciated with bidding creeping up to about $1000. I saw Curt speak to the artist and the artist nod assent. Then Curt interrupted the auctioneer, who a moment later announced Curt would autograph the artwork right then. Bids picked up and the painting sold for a few thousand!

I don't know how much was raised at this event, but I am sure it was a lot. There were hundreds of people there and I think the cost per ticket was $400. (ALS patients who were invited could take additional guests at a discount.)

I can't thank Bonnie enough for engineering this event with Curt. Earlier in the day she even drove in the snow from Taunton to Rockland to feed me lunch. She knew one of my PCAs had called in sick, leaving me without lunch coverage. Thanks to Bonnie's generous act of kindness, I wasn't embarrassed by sounds of my empty stomach growling while Curt Schilling visited with me! It was a fabulous night!

Chapter 29
The Last Month

Lisa gives this account of the events leading up to Linda's last month.

Linda had an annual holiday get together with all of her friends every December. Her condo would be packed to the gills with people. By the fall of 2005, she began to think about whether or not she would be up to having the party that December. She debated for quite awhile about having it. I egged her on and said that it might be the last, so she should do it. Linda always took me into consideration for something like the party because *I* was the one who would be decorating the house and getting all the other mundane stuff in order. One day she was looking through the Avon catalog. Linda always gave little party gifts, and she saw some little soaps in the catalog she really liked. That was the catalyst for her decision to move on with the party!

Whenever she had a special occasion coming along, it was something to look forward to, a diversion from her everyday life because she was making plans. Right after Thanksgiving, we forged ahead into party mode! That really kept Linda going. The party was in early December, and we made it through, but she was totally wiped out afterwards. At night after the party, there was a big breakdown. That was not so unusual, though. Oftentimes when we would have a special event like that (past parties), she would break down when it was over, or a day or two later. It was a release of the all the emotional buildup from the big event. For Linda, it was also a release from the façade she had to maintain for her guests. She would never let on that she was uncomfortable, congested, exhausted, or otherwise while she was entertaining people. She always did a great job projecting the image that she was "just fine."

On Christmas day, my family went over to Linda's early. My sister and her girlfriend Mindy were thrilled that they got to spend some time with Linda. Linda was thrilled as well. Then a short time after we left, Leslie and Norm spent the rest of the day with her.

As per usual, Patty and Garry came to spend New Year's Eve with Linda. I remember I came to put Linda to bed that night, but I told her I had to be back home before 12:00 so I could ring in the New Year with Elaine.

Some time between Christmas and New Year's Linda seemed to be getting more and more congested. Right after the New Year, the congestion got a lot worse, and it appeared she was suffering from a bad cold. We became very reliant on the cough assist and suctioning machines. Of course as soon as we'd clear her up, she'd fill right up again. She was really miserable with this and it was impacting her ability to sleep at night. I was gone for a couple of days, and during that time, her congestion was so bad, she had to sleep in her wheelchair. Even in the chair she barely got any sleep. When I was back after a few days, I spent most of my time with her trying to relieve the congestion. Using the equipment so much was very exhausting for Linda, and it went on like that for a few weeks. She was taking some cold medication, but the cold was getting worse.

On Tuesday, January 17, Linda e-mailed her doctor for the first time to tell him about the severity of her cold. Here is the actual e-mail and the response she received from Dr. Russell's secretary:

Sent: Tuesday, January 17/ 200612:02 PM
To: James Russell
Cc: Avon Printing
Subject; EMERGENCY! VERY SICK, PLEASE HELP!!!

Dear Dr. Russell:

This is urgent and I hope for your quick response via e-mail.

I have no voice for phone communication. I will be alone at home until 5 PM.

New Year's Day I developed a sore throat which developed into a bad, lingering cold. Things have gone rapidly downhill since then.

Symptoms:

Severe respiratory distress for past 4 days
Audible chest wheezing, gurgling, and rattling
Pain and pressure behind my "breastbone"
Can't get a good breath
Constant non-productive coughing
Nausea
Severe headache (something I never get)
Blurry vision
Overall body pain
Chills
Chattering teeth
Overwhelming weakness

I had flu and pneumonia vaccinations in the fall.

My temp is 98.

Yesterday PCA Lisa and I spent repeated sessions with the cough assist and suction, which offered me short, temporary relief. This morning all symptoms are worse than ever.

My local Primary Care provider knows very little about ALS and has never treated me. (I was always seen by his nurse practitioner, who recently left his practice). Past experience at South Shore Hospital has shown they know nothing about ALS.

Should I see you? Should I be in Lahey's hospital with you as the physician overseeing my care? How would this be arranged? You know my position on vents, traches, etc. Could hospitalization help in any way other than resorting to extraordinary measures unauthorized by me?

I am not being dramatic. But I really think I might die very soon, perhaps even today.

PLEASE ADVISE. E-mail me or try calling Lisa Constantino at 781-351-****

Thank you.
Linda Burge

Linda received this response from Dr. Russell's secretary:

Linda, I have spoken to Dr. Russell and he would like you to come directly to the ER here at the Lahey. I have tried to contact Lisa, and I only got her voice mail. Do you have someone else I can call?

Amy

Somehow, Linda had gotten in touch with Gregg – she must have e-mailed him. *(Actually, Linda had cc'd her SOS to Gregg's business e-mail at Avon Printing, hoping he would see it right away and respond to her. Apparently it worked.)* I was working for Faith, a CP patient, and Gregg called me and told me about Linda. I left for Linda's immediately. I called Linda en route. Jackie, an aide, was there, and I said I would be right over. When I got there, Linda told me that Dr. Russell wanted her to go to the Lahey. I said, "Fine. How are we supposed to get there?" She said to call 911 and tell them we needed to be transported to the Lahey clinic. In hindsight I realize you cannot call up 911 and tell them where you want them to take you. Linda had also asked me to call Bill's Taxi. However, I did not feel comfortable taking a sick person in a taxi to Burlington, which was an hour away. I did call 911, and they said that since I had called, though they could not take her to Lahey, they did have to come out to see her and assess the situation. They came out and checked for her oxygen. I think it was at about 83%. It should have been 98-99%. They said Linda's oxygen was too low and they had to transport her to the nearest hospital. Well, Linda went into a raging fit, was screaming obscenities, and wanted the paramedics out of her house. There was no way she would let them take her to the South Shore Hospital. I tried to explain to her that there was *nobody* who could take us to Lahey at that point. I told her that I would not let them admit her to the South Shore Hospital, so she reluctantly agreed to go.

Now while all of this was going on, Linda's friend Barbara was driving down Hingham Street, and saw the ambulance at Linda's condo, so of course she drove in. Somebody came up to me and said there was a woman outside, but she could not come in. So, I went out, saw that it was Barbara, and explained what was happening. I told her to go home and I would call her later.

I rode in the ambulance with Linda. Before leaving, I called Gregg and asked him to meet me at the hospital. I was up front in the ambulance and they would not let me get in back with her. She was frantic in the back. I could see the oxygen mask was blocking her nose, and her arm was wrenched and killing her. Though she was trying to communicate with them, they were not listening to her because she had already established herself as a raving madwoman! Linda was just getting angrier because they were not listening to her, and she realized they would not let me get in back with her. Once at South Shore, they put us in a room, and Gregg showed up. They said they were going to start an IV. Linda made it very clear they were *not* going to start an IV because that would constitute admitting her, and they were NOT going to admit her. We told them to call Dr. Russell who would verify that he wanted Linda at Lahey.

Poor Linda! The entire time her anxiety level was escalating. She was so sick, but had to focus all her energy on getting to Burlington. Then she began to worry that if she ever did make it to Burlington, Dr. Russell might be gone by that time. It was early afternoon at this point, but we spent a couple of hours battling the bureaucracy at South Shore so we could get up to the Lahey. Finally, they reached Dr. Russell, and he asked to speak with me. Dr. Russell asked me to convince Linda that they should start her on an IV at South Shore. I explained to him that she was adamant and there was no way she would relent. I told him that he needed to let the people at South Shore know we had to get Linda to the Lahey or else she would demand to go home. Dr. Russell did get them to agree to send her to Lahey. Now the question became, "What are we transporting her in?" It was finally decided Fallon Ambulance Service would take us to Lahey. Two girls came in to transport Linda – one very heavy girl and one very scrawny girl. Linda told me to help them move her into the stretcher, but they instantly said I could not touch her and I should move away. I realized it was a whole liability thing, so I let them take over, but they barely got her into the stretcher, and I did jump in to help after all. They told me I could ride up front in the ambulance, but I put my foot down and let them know I was riding in the back with Linda. It was now rush hour as we drove to Burlington. We did not have the siren on as we drove, but we made pretty good time.

Before we left in the ambulance, I called Linda's sister Judy to let her know what was going on, and I told her not to come down. There was just too much going on. At that point I was also trying to keep other people at bay who had heard Linda was at the hospital. I did tell Judy that I would call her once we were at the Lahey and knew something.

Linda thought that once we got to Lahey it would be a breeze to get through and then see Dr. Russell. Wrong! They were not set up for us when we got there, and everything seemed like a big deal. First, when we got in, they wanted to get Linda undressed. Linda said "Lisa will do it," but the staff said, "No she won't!" Back to the recurrent battle - Linda did not want me to leave her side and expected me to do whatever I could for her while the staff considered me excess baggage. We were there a half hour when Dr. Russell arrived. His bedside manner under very trying circumstances was superb. He was straightforward with no beating around the bush – just the way Linda preferred. "Linda, you probably have pneumonia. To treat pneumonia we have certain steps we usually follow – IV, antibiotics, sometimes we have to intubate for deep suctioning." Right away Linda said, "No, no, no!" She was quite upset with him.

Dr. Russell clarified that he was not *suggesting* this was the course of treatment for her, but that these were the options available for patients with pneumonia. He was willing to do *whatever* she wanted. He did say that they could not treat the pneumonia aggressively without intubation. Linda said she understood that, but she would not opt for any tubes. Her fear was that if she went that route, she might not be able to come off of a respirator. Dr. Russell agreed to her request and said it would be in the orders.

One of the things I was able to convince her of while she was there was to have a catheter. I told her it just didn't make sense to be asking a nurse every ten minutes to help her with a bed pan. She was initially concerned that she might not be continent again if she had the catheter. I really pushed the comfort factor here, and while she was not thrilled, she did agree to it. They had trouble catheterizing her and they had trouble with the IV, so Linda's perception of the whole ER crew was not the best. She even made a comment to one of the nurses who had trouble inserting the IV about how "unskilled" she was. I know how I would have reacted to such a comment. Yes, it hurts your feelings to have some patient tell you that you're unskilled, but this nurse took it to the next level. "Never in my 20 years of nursing has any patient told me that. I cannot believe you said that!" Now Linda is treating the nurses combatively and she is not making friends! All the while, I am trying to be a mediator. That nurse must have said something to the next nurse who came on, because when she came in she made a comment, and the tension just escalated.

I don't know if there weren't any rooms available or what, but we had to wait in the ER for a long time. While we were waiting, I tried to "entertain" Linda and crack some jokes. She had settled down quite a bit from earlier. Dr. Russell came back at one point while we were still in the ER. He confirmed (after all the tests had been run) that it *was* pneumonia, and that she would be treated for it as she wished. They were going to start her off on antibiotics. Soon after seeing Dr. Russell, they finally took Linda to her room. By this time it was really late – about 11:00 P.M.

Once we did get to the room, it was a whole different story. Linda was treated very well, and I was treated well. They brought a bed in for me. It was a regular twin-size bed - very comfortable. Now that we were in the room, they had to do a full patient assessment. This young guy came in and announced he was a brand new nurse! (One of the things they always told us in nursing school was, don't tell people you are new!) This guy was very cute and Linda liked him…until he was cutting off the South Shore Hospital band from her wrist, and while he was at it, he cut off her **Do Not Resuscitate** (DNR) band as well. Linda went through the roof. She wore that band religiously for many years, and knew that it might be her only means of communication to whomever that she was a DNR – something about which she felt very strongly. She yelled at him for being stupid and careless, and he sheepishly left the room after he had assured Linda that the DNR was already posted. I strolled out of the room to check, knowing full-well what a DNR posting looks like. (Linda had them displayed prominently in her condo.) I didn't see anything, but I did not tell that to Linda. I taped the one he had cut off back around her wrist, and told her that when I went back to her condo, I would get another one and bring it back for her. She settled back down. A little later, the young male nurse came back into the room and apologized profusely to Linda. He was so cute, and told her that he had learned a lesson he would never forget. He would never cut anything off without looking again. It was his mistake and he was very sorry about it. Linda was just fine with him after that.

Neither one of us got much sleep that night. I cough assisted her manually quite a few times, and her breathing did seem a little better. A few times the male nurse came in the room and I held Linda while he performed percussion – slapping her back with his cupped hands. He said he learned it in nursing school, but he had never done it to a patient before. Anyway, it was effective and provided Linda some relief.

Linda and I had talked about people coming to see her. Aside from her family, she really didn't want anybody to see her in the hospital. That was her pride. She didn't want friends to see her when she wasn't at her best, and certainly not when she was sick. She did not want to be remembered like that. Gregg's name came up because he had offered to spend some time at the hospital with her, and because he had been through this with his mom who had died of ALS.

Early the next day, a young nurse's aide came in with all the stuff to clean Linda. She said to Linda, "I am going to give you a bed bath." Linda said, "No you're not. Lisa is going to do it!" I can remember saying, "I thought I was going to get out of it!" So, we laughed about it. I told her I hadn't done this kind of stuff in a long time. It is something you do the first six weeks of nursing school. Once you do it a couple of times in the hospital, you move beyond that. I joked about that, as I got her all cleaned up and looking good for her family's visit.

Judy had called earlier to let Linda know that she, John, and Susan would be at the hospital that day. During that call, I had asked if John could drive me back to the condo so I could get my truck. It was still at Linda's because I had ridden in the ambulance. I felt stranded without having my own transportation there. A short time after they arrived to visit Linda, John drove me back to the condo. Linda had given me a mile-long list of things she wanted me to bring back for her from the condo. I was gone for a couple of hours getting my truck, running a few errands, and making some phone calls to update people on Linda. When I called Leslie, she offered to come to the hospital on Saturday and stay throughout the day and overnight, which would give me another little break. I figured Linda would be fine with Leslie spending the time with her.

After I got back to the hospital, Linda's family was still there. Dr. Russell came in and everyone stayed while he was there. There were some things we wanted to ask Dr. Russell. One of them was "If Linda goes home, what are the options?" I was thinking hospice, but that is not something you could mention to Linda. It was taboo. She equated that with death and the end of the road. Dr. Russell discussed the results of the X-rays they had taken. They found that the left side of her diaphragm was pushed way up and encroaching into the lung area. At the time they thought the bowel was not functioning completely and was also pushing into the same area. Linda was upset that Dr. Russell was explaining all this while Judy and her family were in the room. She felt that was just a little too private. Dr. Russell said they were going to give Linda an enema to see if that relieved the diaphragm problem at all. Then he went into the death and dying thing. He presented her with – this is the course you have chosen, non-aggressive treatment, and I do not know where it's going to go. It may cure the pneumonia, it may not. He told her she had options. She could stop feedings and stop doing everything and say that she had had enough, and he could take measures to keep her comfortable. They give people morphine and drug them up. Well, at that, Linda went nuts. "No, that's suicide and I will not do that!" She was livid. I intervened to help calm her down, and said, "Linda, he is not telling you to do that. He is just making you aware of some options." She was adamant that it was definitely NOT an option for her. Dr. Russell did say that if she wanted pain medication he could put it in the orders, but she said *not* to put it in the orders. Presently the orders called for Tylenol only for pain, plus whatever they were using to thin out the congestion and help her breathing. Linda wanted it kept as such.

It was not too long after Dr. Russell left that Linda's family left as well. They wanted to come back the next day, but Linda said no. That upset Judy because they wanted to be there with Linda. Linda's attitude was to wait because she was hopeful she would be going home soon.

Linda was upset at some of the things Dr. Russell had brought up, but I told her that some of the questions we asked him led right into other areas. It wasn't his fault, and he didn't mean anything by it. Personally, I am glad that certain things got ironed out as far as what Linda would and would not accept. It is just too bad she was overwrought about it.

Between Wednesday and Thursday, I told Linda that I had no plans to desert her, but that my birthday was on Friday and I wanted to wake up in my own bed at my own house on my birthday. She understood and said that was fine with her. I had been with her since Tuesday afternoon and I had gotten little sleep since then. I was not only with Linda, but I was pretty much taking care of all her needs while she was in the hospital as well. It was agreed that Gregg would stay overnight with her while I was gone.

On Thursday we got a surprise visit from Linda's friend Kathy. I don't know how she knew Linda was there. Gail probably called her, but I guess she did not get the message that Linda was not up to seeing anyone. Kathy was coming through town from NH and decided to make a stop to see Linda. When she came to the door she asked if Linda was taking company. What was I supposed to do? I couldn't turn her away. So she came in. She stayed for about 40 minutes, and they actually had a great visit together. They laughed and had a good time.

By this time, they finally had a TV and computer set up in Linda's room. She ended up not using the computer. After Kathy left, Linda asked me to turn "Ellen" on the TV. I told her she already had a lesbian comedian right in front of her! What did she need Ellen for? Linda looked at me and said, "Put Ellen on!" So we just hung out and watched TV for awhile.

Word got around to the nurses by then that Linda had her own care, and they did not have to do much for her. I was on the clock, and I knew that. Linda shared all her meals with me, and I did not have to buy anything. It was like room service! She could order anything at any time.

Somewhere along the line, I was wandering around the floor and looking at the rooms. I noticed the people across the room from Linda had a yellow sticker, as did another room. Then someone else had a green sticker, and Linda had a blue sticker. I thought about when the nurse told me the DNR was posted and I didn't see it. Now it occurred to me that different colored stickers meant different things. I asked Elaine (who had worked in hospitals) and she said that *is* what it was. When I realized that, I did tell Linda, and she was reassured about that DNR posting.

I left Thursday evening around 8:00. Gregg was there and I had to orientate him. He said they had a very peaceful and relaxing night. She spoke to a few people on the phone. I thought she was improving to a point because she was getting treated. She was taking antibiotics and was not as stressed because her needs were being met constantly. After an uneventful night, Gregg left around 10:00 on Friday morning. I had an early birthday dinner with my family on Friday, and I did not get back to the hospital until about 8 PM I thought Gregg was going to stay with Linda until I got back, so I was surprised to learn that Linda had been by herself for most of the day. However, the nurses indicated that she did okay.

When I got back there, I noticed that Linda was drinking from a cup with a straw taped to it. I had never thought of that before!

Linda had two different doctors at Lahey. Dr. Russell was overseeing everything as her ALS doctor. The other was the admitting doctor for the pneumonia. He was doing the treatment for the pneumonia with Dr. Russell's input.

When I got back to the hospital that night, Linda told me that the admitting doctor had told her she was fine, the pneumonia was gone, she was all set, and could go home! I was totally surprised and thinking, "Huh? You still have pneumonia. It's not gone. It's only been two days." Linda was absolutely sure she was going home. To this day, I do not know if he actually said that to her or it was just something she wanted to believe.

A petrified feeling came over me because I had no idea of what we were going to do if Linda came home. I was certainly not ready to become a live-in anything. Linda knew that. Nobody else was prepared to be doing half the stuff we were doing. Now the suctioning was pretty regular, we were doing the breathing treatment every four hours, and she was on oxygen. I did not talk to the doctor, so I knew nothing. I started bringing up my concerns to Linda. For the next four hours we were in the midst of heavy duty conversation which covered a lot of ground. We were so immersed in conversation, that we would not allow any distractions. Some people called on the phone, but I told everyone Linda couldn't talk at that time, and she would call back. At some point, Linda just said, "Don't answer the phone."

The main points of our conversation concerned her homecoming. I told her we had to have things in place for that to happen. I wasn't trying to scare her, but coming home the next day was not realistic because no arrangements had been made to make it work. Other things came up during our long talk. Before Linda had gone into the hospital she had sent me an e-mail that I thought was kind of nasty. She was upset that I did not come over one time when she really needed me, and she laid a big guilt trip on me. At that time I was feeling very pressured that my time was never my own

201

because I would always drop everything and come running whenever Linda called. I did not mention this e-mail to Linda when I first got it. There was too much going on and it just wasn't the time. That night in the hospital our conversation kind of worked its way up to that e-mail, and I brought it up. I said, "What was that all about?" That kind of led to things that were unresolved in our three-year relationship. There was nothing major, but things would come up and her feelings would get hurt, or my feelings would get hurt, and then something else happened and we'd let it go. We never really discussed the issues that were probably trivial in retrospect, but they were still bothersome. At some point in the conversation, Linda said, "Why are we even talking about this?" I had to lie, and said, "Well that's just what we're talking about because that's what came up."

In the back of my head, I recalled learning in nursing school that when some people are dying, there is a natural reprieve, an unconscious effort to get things off their chests. Oftentimes as death is imminent, some people will say things they feel they should have said before, and the process makes them feel energized. I remember that during those four hours Linda was talking as if she was not even sick. Normally, Linda would get fatigued if she talked for 30 minutes straight. I was consciously thinking when she asked why we were discussing the subject at hand if indeed, this was Linda's "natural reprieve" time before death, because it seemed to fit the profile I had learned about in school.

We actually did resolve many little things that came up from that conversation. One of those issues was about scheduling. I always felt that I was the scapegoat because if this one or that one couldn't make their assigned time or started cutting back on their slots, then I was the one who had to fill in. That bothered me, but what could I do? I was the most flexible, so it always came back to me. Though it annoyed me, I did not let on. It was things like that we finally worked out and felt better about when we were through.

I think after four hours of discussion, I had finally persuaded Linda to put off the homecoming for maybe another day. We decided that when we got up in the morning, we'd call the doctors in and get some people in place. I told her she needed to have someone there with her 24 hours a day. She could not stay home alone at night. That bothered her. I hadn't realized what an imposition it was for her to have people spend the night at her condo. It was too great a threat to her independence.

In the hospital that weekend, someone had asked Linda, "Who is with you at night?" and she answered, "I'm alone." The nurses couldn't believe it. Even as uncomfortable as she was at night alone, sometimes, it was still *her* time – her own time – no trespassing. She said she would have felt invaded if people had to spend the night with her at any point. I said to her that I had spent the night, and she said, "No, no, no. Not you!" Yet I do recall that being a big issue with her. I had never realized throughout the three years I was with her that the "invasion" piece was in her head. There were times that I spent the night or other people spent the night for whatever reason. She actually had gotten the sofa bed for when somebody might need to stay overnight. The first time I spent the night was when she had the breast surgery. There were times in the winter when we had bad storms and someone would have to stay over because otherwise, they would not be able to get to Linda's in the morning. However, all of these are examples of overnight stays that were necessary because of emergency situations, and as such, Linda did not consider them threats to her space or privacy.

A nurse had started an IV on Linda when I got there that night because she did not have much to drink during the day. That was about 1,000 CCs of fluid they pumped into her over the course of several hours. That's a lot of fluid, and I am sure it contributed to her congestion. At around midnight, a nurse took out the IV, and we decided to go to sleep and talk about the plans for her to go home in the morning. I was relieved that I had convinced her to postpone going home the next day.

In the four hours Linda and I had been talking, she did not need any suctioning. She was doing fine. Within an hour of the time we lay down to go to sleep, Linda was congested again and trying to clear herself. I began to suction her at about 1:00 A.M. Between 1:00 and 3:00, the congestion was coming quickly, but I was not relieving it enough. I was turning her, suctioning her, and getting all kinds of stuff out. However, she just kept producing more. Those two hours were probably the longest two hours of my life. I kept asking her, "Am I hurting you?" You have to understand that when you continuously pound on someone's chest, you have concerns about physically hurting that person. Linda would always say that she was fine and that I should keep doing it and suctioning. There was a new nurse who had come on around 11:00. She had never worked with an ALS patient before, and had not suctioned a patient before, either. Even though she would periodically come in the room and ask if there was anything she could do, there really wasn't. It was pretty much Linda and me taking care of business. Occasionally the nurse did help me move Linda into a position where she could get a little more oxygen to facilitate her breathing.

In the midst of all the chest compressions and suctioning, Linda said, "My bowels just let loose. That's a sign." Clearly, at that point, she knew the end was near. I tried to make light of it, and said, "Don't worry, we'll clean you up and get you situated, etc." However, I remember thinking that she could be right, but I was hoping she wasn't. We got Linda cleaned up. Later, when she was lying on her side, she calmly said to me, "I think I am going to die. It's okay if I die here." I said, "Are you sure?" She did not have any fear at this point, and was quite composed. She insisted she was okay with it. I told her I would keep doing what I was doing and keep her as comfortable as possible. Linda looked me dead in the eye and she said, "You stay on track. You do what you set out to do, and don't forget. Just keep doing it." (She was referring to my appeal to regain my nursing license, and I was starting school for addiction counseling.) I asked, "And you'll watch over me?" She said, "Yes."

Linda was so peaceful and said she was not afraid. I said *I* was afraid, and I burst into tears. I asked what she wanted me to do, and she told me to hold her hand, which I was already doing. "Can you feel it?" I asked. "Yes. Just stay with me." I told her I did not plan on going anywhere! I still had to get up and down numerous times to suction her and/or make her comfortable.

At some point, she asked me to call Dr. Russell. I had his cell phone number and he had told me to call him at any time. I asked Linda what I would say to him if I called him at 2:00 in the morning. Then I told her that Dr. Russell would most likely ask if she wanted morphine, and what was I supposed to say to that? She thought for a second or two, then said, "Don't call Dr. Russell."

On Tuesday when Linda went into the hospital, she said her body felt different than it ever had before. At that time, I had said to her jokingly, "You are not dying on my birthday (which was three days hence)!" She said she would not do that. In her family, there were quite a few deaths on others' birthdays, anniversaries, etc. At some point, when I was holding Linda and she was fully cognizant, I said, "It's three hours after my birthday. Thank you for keeping your promise and not dying on my birthday!" She smiled.

At times when Linda was having great difficulty breathing and I'd be suctioning her, you could see the panic in her eyes as she gasped for breath. Otherwise, she was composed and amazingly lucid throughout this final journey. After she had accepted her fate and was lying quietly on her side, she said, "Tell my family I love them," and she proceeded to go through a long list of friends to whom the same message of endearment was to be conveyed. Finally I said, "Linda, I will tell them all!" When she started saying these goodbyes to everyone and she had told me to stay on track, that's when I knew that she was serious, and this was her time to go.

It was most likely around 3:00 by this time. It is so hard to tell because the hours between 1:00 and 3:00 seemed to be an eternity. Her breathing became noticeably more difficult. For whatever reason my nursing brain kept thinking, "You've got to know the time of death," so I began watching the clock. The nurse had come in, realized the imminent situation, and asked, "What do we do?" I told her there was nothing we could do because Linda was a DNR. Sometime after 3:00 I told the nurse to call the other nurses

205

because Linda was repeatedly gasping for air. I knew the end was near. I don't even remember how many people came in. At the sight of the other nurses, I just lost it. They said to me, "You're doing everything you can, honey. You just hold her." I had been talking to Linda, so that is what I continued to do. About a minute after the nurses' arrival, Linda passed out. She was still alive, but now she was unconscious, and her heart was still beating. I must have looked at the clock a hundred times between 3:20 and 3:25. The nurses were supporting me as I was holding Linda, and one of them kept listening to her heart until finally she said, "She's gone." It was 3:25 AM - Saturday, January 21, 2006.

Of course I became hysterical, but the nurses stayed with me for awhile. I was still holding Linda, and eventually I calmed down. The nurses left and a new nurse came in for awhile. Then I called Elaine and became hysterical once again. She calmed me down. I did stay in the room quite awhile with Linda. Gregg had brought her a stuffed animal and I propped her up in the bed with the stuffed animal. I didn't know what I should be doing. I called Judy to tell her. She said she already knew. She had a feeling. Judy said she and John would come down later and meet me at Linda's condo. I had no idea what to do. The hospital told me that they needed to know what funeral home would be picking up Linda. Other than that, there was nothing for me to do. The nurse said she was going to clean up Linda to get her ready and asked if I wanted to help. I have never done post mortem care, and I declined. However, it was very difficult for me to leave that room for the last time. I kept going up to her and hugging her body. I became very hyper. I said to myself, "Wow! What did I just go through?" Then there was the disbelief of Linda's passing, which was overwhelming. She and I had been gearing up for that event for three years. "It's going to happen. It's going to happen." Then all of a sudden it happened, and I wasn't ready for it.

I don't think Linda was afraid of dying. Her fear was of being trapped in her body – losing control of her own destiny and losing her independence. Fortunately for her, it never came to that. She still laughed, she still spoke, and she maintained her dignity right up to the end.

206

Chapter 30
After the Shock

I am very grateful that Norm and I spent Christmas with Linda because it was our last day together. It was a lovely afternoon during which we watched a movie ("The Bourne Supremacy") and ate Chinese food. Linda, as always, was very upbeat and positive, and openly delighted that we were spending the day with her. (Norm and I had spent many Christmases with Linda.) At around 5:00, R., another of Linda's health care workers, came with her husband and two young children to visit briefly. Norm and I stayed until about 7:00.

A day or two after our visit, Norm and I traveled to the Berkshires to spend the remainder of the school vacation. About a week or so after we got back, I got an e-mail from Linda telling me that she had gotten a bad cold and it was creating a lot of problems for her. Breathing was difficult and she was having a lot of congestion that was hard to control. A few days later I got another e-mail in which she said that she had resorted to sleeping in her wheelchair in the hope that her position in the wheelchair would be more advantageous for her breathing.

The next thing I knew, Patty called to tell me Linda was in the hospital! Lisa had just called her so she was giving me the news directly. It looked like Linda had pneumonia. The next day I spoke with Lisa and called the hospital and chatted briefly with Linda. I was very relieved to hear that Lisa was staying with Linda 24/7 at the hospital. I told Lisa that I could certainly help out and take a shift and stay overnight. Since school was still in session, all day Saturday and Saturday night would be best for me. Lisa said that would be a real help, so it was settled.

Meanwhile, I spoke with Patty several times during the week. We both agreed this just did not seem like Linda's time to go, and neither of us was ready for that to happen. Of course we were hoping for the best but also realized the severity of an ALS patient suffering from pneumonia.

When I got home from school on Friday, I made some lemon squares to bring to the hospital for Linda. Since I still hadn't heard anything from Lisa or Linda about the arrangements for the next day, I called the hospital at about 8:15. Lisa told me Linda could not come to the phone at that time, and she couldn't talk then either. One of them would call me back later. I went to bed around midnight, not sure about what was going to happen on Saturday because I never got a call back from either Linda or Lisa.

The phone woke me up at 7:30 on Saturday morning. It was a very distressed Lisa. "We lost Linda," she sobbed. I sat bolt upright, in total shock. Lisa gave me some sketchy details and told me that Judy and John would be coming down and meeting her at Linda's condo. I told her I would be over there as well.

When I got there at about 10:30, Judy, John, Lisa, and Linda's friends Patty, Gail, and Barbara were there. We all tearfully hugged each other and talked about what had happened. On one thing we all agreed – that Linda went exactly the way she would have chosen to go. In fact, it was almost as if she had scripted her own departure – in control right up to the very end. Yep, that Linda was one amazing gal!

We talked about when the funeral might be. Of course, Judy would be in charge of all those arrangements. However, Linda already had planned much for her own funeral. About six months previously, she had asked me to give the eulogy at her funeral. I told her I felt honored that she would ask me, and I agreed to do so. I was quite certain that Linda had probably asked several other friends to give eulogies as well. It came as a big surprise to me when I found out on that day (of Linda's death) that I was the only one she had asked. She had also requested that her young friend Amanda sing at her funeral. Linda had bought her burial plot at the same cemetery where her parents rested. And she and Patty had mixed a music tape – several years before – specifically to be played at her wake.

Linda's wake was held in Whitman the following Tuesday, and her funeral was the next day, Wednesday, January 25, 2006 at the Episcopal Church in Whitman. At the church, before the funeral service, as people walked in, there were Scottish bagpipers playing. (Linda had planned this nod to her heritage.) The bagpipers continued until the service began. Amanda's beautiful voice filled the church before the pastor took to the pulpit.

I had spent a long time preparing the eulogy, and as I was doing so, I kept hearing John's (Linda's brother-in-law) voice in my ear, "Keep it short!" I told him I'd try, but it was no use. I had too much to say about Linda that *needed* to be said – about her character, the things that were important in her life, and of course, her battle with ALS, and the remarkable way she handled that struggle.

So many times when people are eulogized, they become larger than life, and their qualities are so exaggerated you wonder if it's the same person. I had no intention of elevating Linda to sainthood and inflating any of her positive traits. I just tried to convey the true essence of Linda as a person, as a friend, and as a woman of intelligence, character, and courage.

The final eulogy was longer that I expected it to be, but I wouldn't change a word. Many people - including John (!) - told me that it was very moving. In my heart, I know Linda would have approved.

The Eulogy:

Family and Friends of Linda-

My name is Leslie and I was a lifelong friend of Linda's. To be completely accurate we actually met in high school. Who would have thought that sharing a gym locker and a love for Richard Chamberlain, TV's Dr. Kildare, would lead to a forever friendship.

But it did. In the more than 40 years that I knew Linda I cannot recall any negative experience or cross words that came between us – ever. It was always smooth sailing, fun, and comfortable.

Friendship was very important to Linda. She was unquestionably a people person and had scores of friends, real friends, not just acquaintances, from all walks of life. As long as you were pleasant, caring, usually well-behaved, and liked to laugh and have fun, then you probably got a ticket into Linda's ever-expanding friendship club.

Linda was the epitome of what every good friend should be. She was kind, extremely thoughtful, considerate, intelligent, had a wonderful sense of humor, and was just plain fun to be with. Linda took a genuine interest in each of her friends, their families, and their activities. She would take great pride in sharing accomplishments of one friend to another. If you needed Linda for anything, she was there to lend her support.

More than anything else, I think Linda would like to have been remembered as a good friend. And I am quite certain that those of us who had the good fortune to be counted among Linda's friends, consider it a privilege to have known and loved her for so many years.

In the past year I have been chronicling Linda's battle with ALS, and we have had many discussions about how she has dealt with this disease.

When Linda was diagnosed with ALS in 1999, it was an absolute shock to everyone. She was not going to get better. Lou Gehrig's disease is *always* fatal. Still, Linda *was* hopeful. She was realistic enough to know that she was not going to improve or be cured, but she had every expectation that she would live life to the fullest for as long as she possibly could. Linda was not going to allow a devastating diagnosis to interrupt her full life. She was going to fight back and fight back hard for as long as possible.

Linda was a true "profile in courage" throughout her battle with ALS. She was a super-sharp, articulate advocate for herself, which,

210

on countless occasions, helped her navigate through numerous bureaucratic roadblocks. She was fiercely independent and fought hard to maintain her status living alone. She faced this hideous disease with the most remarkable grace and acceptance. Amazingly, despite everything she went through, Linda *never* complained and there was *never* an inkling of self pity. She refused to see herself as a victim.

When Linda had been battling ALS for almost a year she was already making numerous accommodations in order to function like a "normal" person. One day we were discussing how she had been able to continue her normal lifestyle, including working full time, with these modifications, and when I told her that I thought she was quite incredible, her response was that she was "just another woman living her life, facing its challenges to the best of her ability..." I begged to differ with her response, and insisted that she was a <u>remarkable</u> woman who was living every moment <u>overcoming</u> the challenges that had been heaved in her path.

Granted, there are many others who face serious illness and overcome obstacles thrown before them, but few, if any, take on their battle armor, or are even capable of doing so, in the manner that Linda did. First and foremost, that persistent positive attitude of hers pervaded *everything* she did. She did not dwell on things she couldn't do, but modified whatever she had to in order to achieve the desired result. She was human and had her share of frustrating moments, but she would never complain about them to others.

Linda, always the independent person, was not about to sacrifice that independence for anything – not even ALS. She was nothing if not realistic, so she was well aware that she would not be able to maintain the level of independence to which she was accustomed. However, there was no way she was going to a nursing home or any other facility where she was not in charge of her own fate.

For awhile, Linda managed with the accommodations she made to continue living in her normal manner. However, ALS keeps chipping away, bit by bit, chunk by chunk, at one's independence.

Ultimately, Linda had to stop driving and get someone else to take her to and from work everyday. She finally had to stop working the day that she could no longer negotiate the one step necessary to get into her office.

She began using a cane, that progressed to a walker, and that progressed to a wheelchair.

Linda's intelligence and perseverance guided her game plan for ALS. She educated herself about the disease and realized early on that she had to plan ahead for future contingencies in her daily living activities. She told me, "I am running a race I will not win, but I've tried to stay in the race. A very big part of that is being proactive rather than reactive." It made all the difference in her quality of life. There were so many little modifications that she made to her daily routines – changing her round door knobs to elongated ones, putting wire loops on drawer handles so they could be opened, and using a special cutting board. These are but a few of the hundreds of little changes that were made. One of the frustrations of this disease is that sometimes, in a matter of a day, your ability to do something can disappear. Linda told me that one morning she could turn on a light switch, but four hours later, she could not do that same task – and she could never do it again.

Another proactive step Linda made at just the right time was moving into a one-level condo without any stairs to worry about. At the time Linda ordered her electric wheelchair, she needed no more than a basic electric wheelchair. However, Linda, always thinking ahead, made sure the chair was fitted with accommodations that she would need a year or two hence, when her disabilities became more severe.

Eventually, Linda did need the assistance of health care workers. It started off slowly, but escalated to more and more care. This was definitely preferable to a nursing home. As long as Linda could remain in her condo, she felt in control of her life. At one point, however, when Linda realized she not only needed more care, but she needed more *skilled* care, she despaired that barring a full time nurse, which she could not afford, she would not be able to find anyone who could provide that skilled care. Enter Linda's real life guardian angel. That's when Lisa Constantino came into Linda's life. Both of these women were at a crossroads in their lives. They became each other's salvation. Their bond was ironclad and impenetrable. Linda's desire to help Lisa gave her a sense of purpose beyond her fight with ALS. Lisa's newfound sense of purpose was not only to be Linda's primary caregiver and oversee all other caregivers, but to help in every conceivable way to prolong Linda's quality of life. Linda and Lisa became endearing friends and confidantes and shared a steadfast, caring, and loving relationship that enriched both of their lives. They were totally devoted to each other, and I know I am one of many who is so thankful to Lisa because she not only extended Linda's quality of life, but I truly believe she also gave us more time with Linda.

Throughout all the trials and tribulations she encountered in the past seven years, Linda managed to make her life as normal as possible. Almost everyone else would have resigned themselves to bed permanently. It is much easier. But Linda wasn't looking for the easy way out. She was adamant about getting out of that bed every single day, getting bathed and dressed, in a routine that could take up to two hours, and facing the day with her various activities – answering e-mail, taking care of her banking online, reading, doing physical therapy, chatting with company, watching a video, or whatever. She never lacked for things to do. This allowed her some semblance of normalcy.

Though Linda accepted this daily routine, she sometimes ached to escape from the walls of her tiny condo. Thank goodness for Ron Hoffman's Compassionate Care van program. Through this service, Linda could borrow the van for up to a week at a time and take off for parts unknown. So the dynamic duo – Linda and Lisa – would plan their itinerary of places to go and people to see when they had the van. Linda was so exhilarated by the opportunity to get out into the world, visit friends, go shopping, drive to the ocean. It was at these times that she could *almost* forget she had ALS. That van was a godsend, and the van adventures of the infamous duo were major highlights in Linda's last few years.

Despite Linda's ever increasing disabilities, she had the busiest social life of anyone I know. As I said earlier, Linda had legions of friends, and she was fond of saying after she got ALS that there was not a deserter in the bunch! She also attracted a bevy of more friends in the years after her diagnosis. People were always popping by her condo to visit and chat or bring over some food. Unlike the typical visit with most people who have a serious illness, a visit with Linda was *always* an uplifting experience. That is why she had so much company. Linda made sure her guests were comfortable. She did not talk or complain about her illness and turned the conversation to her guests. She was more than content to listen to others talk about themselves or their families. Social visits were filled with lots of laughter, and Linda thrived on them.

I have asked myself so many times how Linda was able to get through all of the obstacles she had to face on a daily basis. I do know that her sense of humor was instrumental in helping her throughout her entire illness. She could find something to laugh about in almost every imaginable situation. I would like to share one funny story with you that Linda related to me about a time when she was first dealing with ALS. These are Linda's words:

Looking back on it, it's a laughable experience, but at the time, it was scary. I was still living in the townhouse condo, and normally I showered, but one afternoon I got it in my mind, "Wouldn't a long soak in the tub be nice!" Well it was almost a *lifelong* soak in the tub! I filled the tub, I climbed in, I soaked, I enjoyed it thoroughly, I got ready to get out, drained the tub, went to stand up, and could not get to my feet. There were no bars in that tub, but nothing would have helped. I could not stand. So, I tried to be calm and I thought, "Okay, breathe, gather your strength, you can do this."

Now it was summertime and the room was not cold, but I was wet and naked, and chilling rapidly. So, what I decided to do was turn the water back on and warm up, then drain it out and try again. Up until that time, if I were on the floor, I could get back to my feet, so I assumed that in the tub I could get to my feet. I drained the tub again, and with all the confidence I had, I attempted to get to my knees at least. No – could not get out of that tub. Ultimately, I ended up - with every bit of strength that I had, literally swinging myself out onto the floor. I flopped over the side of the tub. Like a beached whale, I was now wet and cold on a tile floor. Somehow, I managed to crawl on my hands and knees to the toilet and use the base to pull myself up. I remember I sat on the toilet and I first started to cry, and then I was laughing. I remember just laughing and laughing, and thinking I would be the $10,000 prizewinner on America's Funniest Home Videos! When I finally had the strength, I managed to walk into my bedroom, climb on the bed and pull the covers over me. I was shivering. Ultimately, I recouped and got dressed. I called my friend Gail, and I said to her "I have just taken the last tub bath I will ever have." It was comical by then, but it also was like a revelation or a realization of the future, and it struck me with a lot of force that my life was changing rapidly and drastically.

That story speaks volumes because it not only shows how her sense of humor truly helped her survive a terrifying situation, but it's also an example of Linda's remarkable strength of character. She did not panic, she coolly assessed her options and literally willed herself out of that tub. Then later she was able to reflect on the experience and realize the formidable ramifications.

When Linda went into the hospital last week, Patty Baylor and I talked about how we were not ready for Linda to go yet, and of course, we were hoping that she would rally and be okay. Truthfully, I don't think we would ever be ready for our dear friend to go, but Linda knew it was time because even if she had rallied, her quality of life would never have been the same. And that was the most important thing to her. We are all so grateful and it gives us such comfort that she was with Lisa in her final hours of life. Linda, who always had to be in control, made sure the script called for her to be in the arms of her guardian angel when she peacefully passed on.

Almost six years ago, I wrote something to Linda that applies tenfold today. I said:

Linda, you are an amazing inspiration to anyone who knows you, and you have certainly set the standard for courage and dignity in the face of unrelenting obstacles. Somehow, I doubt that anyone else could meet that same standard. I am in awe.

How fortunate and how truly privileged we all were to know the amazing Linda Laird Burge.

Linda, you were one in a million. We love you. May you always rest in peace.

****

I cannot conclude a summary of the funeral without mentioning a comic interlude. After the funeral service at the church, a lot of people decided to make the 40 mile (one way) ride to the cemetery in Peabody. Norm and I had come in separate cars, as he had to go to work after the service. Patty was going to ride with me in my car to the cemetery. We ended up following Lisa, her girlfriend Elaine, and Lisa's daughter Chelse. Elaine was driving. At a stop at a red light, Lisa got out of the car, went around to the other side and did something, then got back in. Patty and I did not know what that was all about, but they were ready to move when the light changed. After we were traveling for quite awhile, we saw Elaine pull over to the side of the road. We looked at them as we passed, thinking, what is this shenanigan? At this point we were behind Judy and John, who were right behind the hearse. Shortly thereafter, Judy and John turned left, while the hearse kept going straight. Pat and I thought that strange, but we decided to stay behind the hearse because they couldn't do anything without Linda! However, we looked at our directions and knew we were well beyond the cemetery. After a couple of miles, the hearse pulled into the breakdown lane and we followed. The driver got out and asked if we knew where we were because clearly, they were lost! We showed them the directions, issued by their funeral home (!) and said we needed to turn around and go back in the other direction. The driver agreed, and we finally got there – the last to arrive! The others could not imagine what had happened to poor Linda! When

216

Patty and I saw Lisa, we asked why they had pulled off the road earlier. Their car broke down! Patty and I felt terrible – we had NO idea. If the earlier episode at the red light hadn't happened, we probably would have pulled in behind them, but we thought they were up to some crazy business again. Fortunately, another car in our funeral cortege pulled over to rescue them. They returned home with us and had their car towed.

Judy thought about what to do after the funeral service and the cemetery. At one point she was going to have those who came to the cemetery go to a restaurant with them, but in the end, she was not comfortable with that or with anything else on the funeral day. In lieu of a gathering at that time, she decided to wait a few months and then have a little get together for family and friends at a restaurant closer to Linda's condo.

About five months later, in May, 2006, close to the time of what would have been Linda's 59th birthday, Judy hosted a luncheon gathering in memory of Linda at a restaurant in Rockland. Lisa and her mom made most of the arrangements, and it worked out quite well. About 30 people were able to come.

Very informally, after lunch, people voluntarily stood up to talk about how Linda had made an impact on their lives, or to share some kind of Linda story. It was lovely and very heart warming. However, everyone was brought to tears when Shauna – one of Linda's young health care workers – spoke. She got very emotional and said that Linda was the first positive female role model she had had in her life, which was something she appreciated dearly. She learned so much from Linda, and would always listen to and try to heed her thoughtful advice.

As everyone was dabbing their eyes with tissues, Mary Beth, another of Linda's young health care workers, got up and herself teary eyed, related that Linda had been instrumental in helping her get out of an abusive, negative relationship in her life. She would never forget how Linda's words helped her gain the strength to do what she needed to do. Like Shauna, she looked up to Linda as a positive female role model.

There were people at that luncheon ranging in age from early 20s to early 90s; professionals, blue collar workers, and retired people. Linda's friends were from every class and from every age group, and she touched all of them.

Chapter   31
Living with ALS

There wasn't one person in Linda's retinue of friends who did not take notice of the gallantry of her handling and management of ALS. From the outset, Linda's attitude was to deal matter-of-factly with all the related issues and incidentals of the disease so she could move on with her life. She was totally aware of the devastation this illness would wreak on her body as time progressed, but she was determined to deal with it one day at a time. Linda would be a person "living with ALS," not "dying from ALS." That was a most important distinction for her.

Linda wanted to be as "normal" as possible under the circumstances. That is why she continued to work full time for a long as she possibly could. That is why, though it took two hours to get up, bathed, and dressed everyday, she did it. That is why she found alternative ways of doing things that had become physically impossible for her. That is why she did not want to have anything at all to do with a nursing home. That is why when one doctor recommended she have permanent catheterization strictly for the sake of convenience, she was incensed, and adamantly refused. That is why whenever people came over to visit, the topic of discussion was *never* ALS, but usually mundane girl talk, or a subject having to do with the guest.

Linda made the best of the hand she was dealt. However, she did it with the most incredible grace and dignity that one could imagine. As her friends, we were all in awe of how she was able to truly appreciate her life and the little things that most of us take for granted – nature, music, books, friends, etc. Many people who suffer with fatal progressive diseases seem to resign themselves to misery and self-pity. That was the antithesis of Linda.

My admiration for the way Linda conducted herself throughout her illness never ceased growing. In the first year after her diagnosis, I made several aborted attempts to write a letter, just to let her know that I considered her an inspiration, and a true role model. In response to one of Linda's letters to me - she was always a great letter writer - I ultimately did express to her how I felt.

Unbeknownst to me (until years later), her best friend Patty Baylor had also written a similar letter to Linda five months prior to mine. I will duplicate that letter here (with the exception of the first paragraph which dealt with an extraneous matter).

March 25, 2000

Hello Again!

... Speaking of high regards, I want to tell <u>you</u>, how much I admire <u>your</u> attitude. I wouldn't call it "cavalier" at all, but rather courageous. How fortunate, how blessed I feel to have you as my friend – you have always been a role model for me and taught me so much throughout our many years together. Do you know, I can't remember us ever having a quarrel, can you?

It occurred to me after our conversation on the way back to your home that you might have thought that I have a "cavalier attitude" toward your illness, because we were keeping the tone philosophical rather than personal, but I hope you know that my heart aches for you – and for all of us who love you. We are all trying to deal with your illness as best we can, and you, dearest friend, are showing us the way. I can't imagine a time without you being there for me, but I know that I'll <u>always</u> be able to talk to you, just as you do to your mom and dad.

Thank you so much for being my <u>very</u> <u>best</u> <u>friend</u> for so much of our lives.

You are such an incredible person – I hope you realize that!

With all my love and prayers,
Pat

****

My letter followed in August of the same year.

August 24, 2000

Hi Linda-

Got your recent note, and felt I had to respond. (Believe it or not, I still remember going over to your house and cooking for you, but who knows if it will still be in my head tomorrow!!!)

First of all, you need not send me "thank you" notes for anything. I know that it is a real effort for you to do. Though it is a formality your good manners have always dictated you do, circumstances have changed. I know you appreciate anything that is done for you, and I hope you can accept that a verbal "thank you" is all that is necessary. And forgive me here if this sounds like I was doing some kind of a task for you, because I certainly was not. It was a REAL pleasure for me to spend the time with a cherished friend. That it was helpful to you was an added bonus.

Now I also want to re-address our little discussion of how you have coped with your illness. What I said to you is part of what I had tried to put to paper several months ago. In fact, I was hoping to have a little tome to give you at the time of our birthday get together. Though I had several pages written, it was beginning to sound too maudlin, so I abandoned it at the time, but hoped to edit it. Busy girl that I am, that did not happen, so I will try again now.

The point that I wanted to make in my previous attempt, and what I hinted at when we were together, is that I think you are extraordinary, truly extraordinary. Yes, I know you are a strong person, and always have been. But Linda, being a strong person does not guarantee amazing grace while facing extreme adversity (on a daily basis).

You said that I made you feel special (You are!!), "successful somehow. But I know I'm not. I'm just another woman living her life, facing its challenges to the best of her ability..."

Linda, are you kidding?????? You have been INCREDIBLY successful in your battle against this disease so far. You have been able to maintain a great degree of independence (with a wonderful support system), continue to work, live in your own condo, take care of yourself, enjoy a social life, and retain a keen sense of humor as well as a positive outlook and perspective on your life. You most certainly are NOT "just another woman living her life, facing its challenges to the best of her ability..." You are a remarkable woman who is living every moment overcoming the challenges that have been heaved in your path. DO NOT underestimate your courage and the choices you have made to deal with this.

I truly believe that most people in your situation would take the road of least resistance. Most wouldn't continue working, and would find it a lot easier to sit home, collect disability and feel sorry for themselves. Under the circumstances, who would blame them? When life deals you a rotten hand, totally unexpectedly, from which there is no escape, it stinks. Almost any such reaction would be considered justified.

It is a hell of a lot more difficult to stick it out and fight tooth and nail before being forced down for the count. It takes guts, discipline, determination, stamina, will power, courage, and fortitude.

As I said to you before, we all wonder how we would react if confronted with extreme adversity. While many of us would like to *think* we'd be models of grace under pressure, the fact is we do not *know* unless we are actually hit with the reality.

I, too consider myself a strong person. I have often wondered what I would do if I were faced with a similar situation. I'd like to think that I would not pity myself or give up, but try to carry on as best I could, being as self sufficient as I could. But alas, would I really? I am not so sure. Faced with the reality, my frustration level might be a lot lower than I'd expect. Who knows - there are just so many variables that enter into the equation that I couldn't even fathom UNLESS I was actually in that reality.

I absolutely meant it when I said I am in awe of you and the way you have dealt with this. Even in my wildest imaginings of my hypothetical adversity, I would never be able to conjure up the strength of spirit and perpetual optimism that you exhibit. (Maybe, in retrospect, it's not so surprising that doctor of yours wanted to suggest psychological counseling - not because YOU needed it. But rather, because everyone else he sees needs it, as they simply cannot cope with the physical and emotional demands of the disease. Does this make sense to you?) I really, really believe that you are an anomaly, and I mean that in the most complimentary way.

We have always been good, close friends, Linda. I have always had a lot of respect for your intelligence, kindness, sincerity, sense of humor and generosity, and I believe they are the qualities that brought us together as friends in the first place (in addition to our mutual adoration of Richard Chamberlain!!). In the past year and a half, despite your physical limitations, you have climbed to the top of the pedestal, and I am straining my neck just to look at you!!

I understand why you feel that "God keeps" you "in his care," but Linda, YOU'RE the one doing all the work here!!!!!!.....and YOU deserve the credit!!!!!

You are an amazing inspiration to anyone who knows you, and you have certainly set the standard for courage and dignity in the face of unrelenting obstacles. However, I doubt that any of us could meet that same standard. And that, my friend, is why I am "in awe!"

222

With much love,
Leslie

****

These letters obviously meant a lot to Linda. When I helped her put together a scrapbook of her "ALS Career," she wanted both letters on the first couple of pages.

Not everyone is equipped to handle an illness like ALS in the manner Linda did. For one thing, most people have a significant other, a parent, or a son or daughter who can assume a caretaker's position – looking after the patient and making major decisions. Linda did not have the luxury of a significant other, parent, or child who could have done that for her. However, that probably worked in her favor. Linda had always been extremely independent, so it was not a stretch for her to be proactive and take on the responsibility for her disease management, deal with the bureaucracy when it set up roadblocks, and keep as informed as possible to stay a step or two ahead of her illness. She had no blueprint to guide her along her journey. She blazed the path as she ventured along from one new territory to another – health care workers, insurance, kitchen equipment, bathroom equipment, wheelchairs, lifts, Lifeline, technological equipment, social security, etc. It was not easy, but Linda was persistent. On many occasions, Linda would spend whole days researching, investigating, and planning some aspect of her ALS management.

Though staunchly independent, Linda realized early on that she would have to accept the assistance of many others if she wanted to continue living by herself. At first it was getting a ride to and from work when she could no longer drive. Then it was a few friends who helped her get up and dressed in the morning and into bed at night. It escalated to more and more health care workers as her needs continued to grow. Ultimately, Linda had numerous people traipsing in and out of her condo all day long to support her daily living. Friends often brought meals for Linda's well-stocked freezer, went on shopping errands, or made banking runs for her.

From beginning to end, she was able to live alone, and be in total control – a major victory for Linda.

It's ironic that "it took a village" for Linda to retain her independence throughout her battle with ALS, but she wouldn't have had it any other way. Because Linda was able to be in control throughout the duration of her disease, she did not have to compromise her quality of life – a factor of extreme importance to her. That is why Linda's story of her journey through ALS is a celebration of the triumph of her indefatigable spirit.

Acknowledgements

This book could never have been written without the consent and cooperation of Linda Burge herself. Her story begged to be told, and I am most grateful that she was a willing subject and participant. In reality, she co-authored much of this story. I merely put her words to print (and provided additional information). I truly hope that I have done justice to her incredible journey through the minefield of ALS.

My sincere appreciation is also extended to Patty Baylor, Lisa Constantino, and Judy Gilman for sitting through hours of interviews and editing the transcripts of those interviews to share their relationships with Linda. Each of them played a significant role in Linda's life, and their input was invaluable to her story.

Special thanks to Patty who spent much time editing the completed story and making suggestions for improvements. I am greatly indebted to her for her generous efforts and enthusiastic support of this project.

Thanks to Dan Hyman for his expertise in helping put the cover together for this book.

Lastly, I again thank my dear friend Linda, for being my real-life role model and inspiration. Linda, your journey through ALS taught me things that have affected me profoundly. I am grateful for all the treasured memories of our many years of friendship, and I will cherish them forever.

Resources

These are the resources Linda used and benefited from most frequently.

Compassionate Care ALS
Ron Hoffman, Executive Director
P.O. Box 1052
West Falmouth, MA 02574
(508) 563-3677
www.ccals.org

CCALS provides holistic support to ALS patients and caregivers. They give advice, help with equipment needs, and offer a welcome presence of emotional support throughout a patient's ALS journey.
***
ALS Family Charitable Foundation
P.O. Box 229
Buzzards Bay, Massachusetts 02532
508-759-9696
www.alsfamily.org

The ALS Family Charitable Foundation raises funds for research and patient services. They sponsor the yearly "Cliff Walk," a major fundraiser for ALS in which "Linda's Lucky Charms" have participated since 2003.
***
ALS Association
Massachusetts Chapter
320 Norwood Park South
Second Floor
Norwood, MA 02062
1-888-CURE-ALS
www.als-ma.org

The MA ALS Chapter offers more than a dozen free services for patients and their families, including a respite care program, an equipment loan program, a children's program and support groups.

***

Everyday Life with ALS: A Practical Guide
This book is published by the Muscular Dystrophy Association. It is the single best resource for all aspects of everyday living with ALS.
An absolute <u>must</u> for anyone diagnosed with ALS.

www.als-mda.org/publications/everydaylifeals/

***

KNOX-BOX Rapid Entry System
KNOX-BOX (A key to your house is kept in a locked box outside your home for emergency access by the Fire Department) For more info:
www.knoxbox.com

***

Lifeline Medical Alert Service
1-800-797-4191
www.lifelinesystems.com

There are many other resources available online, including:

***

MDA (Muscular Dystrophy Association) ALS Division
www.als.mdausa.org

***

MDA/ALS Newsletter Magazine
Current and back issues available online for magazine with the latest info about everything ALS.
www.als.mdausa.org/publications/als/als-curr.html